cop. a

B   Morgan, Kathryn L.

Children of
   strangers

DATE			

9x-6/04
9/06

Ⓑ THE BAKER & TAYLOR CO.

Children of Strangers

Children of Strangers
The Stories of a Black Family

Kathryn L. Morgan

Cap. a

Temple University Press   Philadelphia

Library of Congress Cataloging in Publication Data

Morgan, Kathryn L
    Children of strangers.

    Includes bibliographical references.
    1. Morgan, Kathryn L.   2. Gordon family.   3. Afro-
American folk-lore—Pennsylvania—Philadelphia.
4. Afro-Americans—Pennsylvania—Philadelphia—Biog-
raphy.   5. Philadelphia—Biography.   I. Title.
F158.0.N4M67   974.8'1100496073 [B]   80-21144
ISBN 0-87722-203-7

Temple University Press, Philadelphia 19122
© 1980 by Temple University. All rights reserved
Published 1980
Printed in the United States of America

To my mother Maggie

Contents

Photographs

Acknowledgments

The first part of this volume was rewritten and published in 1966 at the urging of Professor Kenneth Goldstein of the Folklore and Folklife Program at the University of Pennsylvania. It was Professor Goldstein who first recognized in this work something of value. I wish to thank him and his wife Rochelle for their help and encouragement.

Parts of Part I and the Preface are revisions of material originally published as "Caddy Buffers: Legends of a Middle Class Negro Family in Philadelphia," Keystone Folklore Quarterly II (Summer 1966): 67–88, and are reprinted by permission.

It is my pleasant duty to thank Alan Dundes, professor of anthropology and chairman of the graduate program in folklore at the University of California at Berkeley for his invaluable suggestions, for his support and encouragement, and for his interest in my research over the years. To Lawrence Levine, professor of history at Berkeley, thanks are due for his reading of the draft of the manuscript. I wish to express my gratitude, too, to Ralph Renzler and Bess Lomax Hall of the Smithsonian Institution, along with Stephen Zeitzler of the Family Folklore Program of the Smithsonian, for their encouragement.

To the research team from the Educational Film Center, who conducted formal interviews with my mother and other members of my family, I must give special commendation. Their intensive field work in connection with the recording, filming and dramatization of selected versions of the stories from the published essay as part of a pilot film for "The Storytellers" was impeccable.

The idea of writing two additional sections supplementing the first part, and bringing them together in one volume, came about through the suggestion of my colleague Harrison Wright, chairman of the Department of History at Swarthmore College. Professor Wright also read each section and offered many other valuable suggestions and criticisms as I was writing the second and third parts during the summer of 1976 and the summer and fall of 1978.

During the course of my work I received critical comments and additional critical perspectives from my black colleagues and fellow folklorists, Professor Gerald Davis of Rutgers University at Livingston and Professor Beverley Robinson of the University of California at Los Angeles.

I extend my thanks to Professor Emeritus Hilde Cohn of the German Department at Swarthmore College, to Mrs. Adeline Silverman of Swarthmore, Pennsylvania, and to Professor Barbara Gates of the English Department at the University of Delaware. Through their sensitive reading of the manuscript in its roughest forms I received many helpful suggestions and much needed moral support.

I especially wish to thank Mrs. Sarah Fought for her careful editing and typing of the manuscript.

I thank my daughter, Susan, for helping me shape her into a full-fledged traditional family storyteller at the age of ten.

I appreciate the grant from the American Philosophical Society in the summer of 1971 that helped finance field work in the collection of additional materials. I wish also to express my thanks to Swarthmore College for the research grant that helped finance the editing and typing of the manuscript.

Last but not least I wish to give special thanks to my mother Maggie for all her teachings over the years. I have benefited from these legends all my life.

Preface

Our folklore was the antidote used by our parents and our grandparents and our great-grandparents to help us counteract the poison of self-hate engendered by racism.

Like many black families, the Gordons grew up in the South, where, according to a Southern folklorist:

> The child is introduced to racial prejudice early in his life. The names which he hears applied to the Negro such as "coon," "darky," "Nigger," and "burr head" give an early impression that the Negro is an object of humor and scorn. He buys fireworks called "nigger chasers," nuts called "nigger toes," makes a toy called a "nigger shooter," and recites a jingle about catching "a nigger by his toe." [1]

There is a tie that binds us all no matter what our education, socio-economic status, hair texture or skin color. If we are known to be black, we have experienced in some degree the humiliations common to blacks throughout the United States. It is traditional among black American parents to struggle time and time again to reduce prejudice to fit the understanding of their children.

Martin Luther King describes such moments in "Letter from Birmingham Jail" as times

> when you suddenly find your tongue twisted and your speech stammering as you seek to explain to your six-year-old daughter why she can't go to the public amusement

park that has just been advertised on television, and see the tears welling up in her eyes when she is told that Funtown is closed to colored children, and see the ominous clouds of inferiority beginning to distort her personality by develop-ing an unconscious bitterness toward white people. . . .[2]

Saunders Redding describes how he felt when he tried to ex-plain to his six-year-old son why the little white boy would not play with him anymore:

In his eyes was the look of a wound and I knew how it could grow and become infected and pump its poison into every tissue, to every brain cell. I did not know how to deal with it. Words were poultices to seal the infection in. I could recall them from my own childhood in answer to "why." For children are not born with answers.[3]

And Ernest J. Gaines presents this dialogue between a black woman and a black teenager:

I hope they all aren't like me, the boy said. Unfortunately I was born too late to believe in your God. Let's hope that the ones who come after will have your faith if not in your God, then in something else, something that they can lean on. I haven't anything. For me, the wind is pink; the grass is black.[4]

The "something else" for us was the family legends centering around my great-grandmother, affectionately known to us as "Caddy." Caddy legends have served as "buffers" from racism for the children in our family for four generations. Although there are many similar narratives[5] in folk histories dealing with the ordeals of slavery, with its whippings, rapes, murders, es-capes and pursuits, they did not belong to us, as did the legends of Caddy. The other narratives along with the spirituals finally belonged to the world, but Caddy was ours.

She was among the first generation of freed blacks. The struggle for survival in the remnants of a slave economy was difficult for her because she was alone, illiterate and unskilled. She also had two very young children, conceived by former slaveholders, she had to care for. Her children, Albert and Adeline, were born enslaved and were freed along with her when they were about three and four years old. Adeline died at an early age but Albert, who became my grandfather, worked along with Caddy in Lynchburg, Virginia, until he met and married Kate, who became my grandmother.

When Kate was an infant, her white father sold her away from her mother into slavery. She knew neither her mother nor her father. Both Kate and Albert were unskilled and illiterate; they worked along with Caddy to help buy property and save money to enable the children of the third generation to go to school. The children were my mother Maggie, her sisters Rosebud and Adeline, and her brothers Prince, Jimmie, Benny and William. There were other members of our family in Lynchburg including numerous cousins, uncles and aunts.

In 1915 and 1916 selected members of the family who could pass for white were sent north to Philadelphia to explore the possibilities for employment for themselves and other members of the family able to "pass." Those who could not pass remained in Lynchburg and worked at whatever odd jobs they could find. My mother Maggie, one of the members able to pass, was sent to Philadelphia each summer during her vacation to visit her sisters, both of whom were passing.

She met and married my father during one of her summer excursions, and as a result we had the dubious distinction of being the first generation born in the North. My father, who was in school when he married, left school and worked as a postal clerk. My mother struggled patiently to raise the children, brow-beat the landlords, and made the money stretch by preparing nourishing but inexpensive Southern meals.

She always attempted to instill in us some sense of honor and dignity, which in her estimation would help us survive in this unnatural Northern vacuum between the black and white worlds. Both parents attempted to destroy by example and discipline the stereotype of black Americans that was constantly before us as children. The creature of stupid hangdog expression, lazy-lipped mumbling speech, bug-eyed look, white teeth, gaudy clothes, and hunched-over walk was hated with a passion in our house.

There was no denying that Hattie McDaniel and Louise Beavers, the perennial maids and mammies of the movies, were the female stars of the day, and Stepin Fetchit (Lincoln Perry), with his eye-rolling, bewildered expression, head-scratching and dropping dialect, the most popular black motion picture personality in the country. In school we were reading about "Little Black Sambo," and our textbooks were chockful of disparaging things about blacks and their African background. The lies that blacks were inferior and that slaves were sleek, well-fed and happy under the patronizing and loving "ole Massa" had not yet been destroyed by the social scientists. As our teachers were all white, we learned no black history in school. There was no evidence in our schoolbooks that blacks had any part at all in building this great democracy. Many parents in our neighborhood were distressed by this image and proceeded to set the children's teeth on edge by trying to make them into carbon copies of the typical white middle-class Protestant American boy and girl. James Baldwin vividly describes the results of such parental concern:

> One's hair was always being attacked with hard brushes and combs and Vaseline; it was shameful to have "nappy" hair. One's legs and arms and face were always being greased, so that one would not look "ashy" in the wintertime. One was always being scrubbed and polished as though in the hope that a stain could be washed away. I hazard to say that the Negro children of my generation, anyway, had an earlier and more painful acquaintance with soap than any other

children anywhere. The women were forever straightening and curling their hair and using bleaching creams. And yet it was clear that none of this effort would release one from the stigma and danger of being a Negro; this effort merely increased the shame and rage. There was not, no matter where one turned, any acceptable image of oneself, no proof of one's existence.[6]

This was the world of books and movies—a world of Goldilocks and Shirley Temple curls. Is it any wonder that accounts of black history and family valor were fervently passed down by word of mouth from generation to generation?

There is something very personal about writing about the members of one's family when one is a so-called "middle-class" black American. It is like having a second self which urges one to "polish up" the English, overdramatize the positive values expressed in the lore, and suppress facts which may reflect negatively on the family image or contribute to stereotypes of black Americans. But I have tried to let the stories, as told, speak for themselves.

I believe that contemporary assessments of black family life cannot afford to ignore legends like these. The black writer John O. Killens is right when he states that "Richard Wright was never closer to the truth than when he spoke of the strength of familial love" in black family groups.[7] While this statement may not hold up in light of what has been *written* about black family life by academics and others, W. E. B. Du Bois had already warned against concentrating on the written word alone. For, as he notes, the deeds and thoughts of men that have been accurately written down are as pinpoints in the sea of human experiences.[8]

My family stories and similar stories collected from other black families can be viewed in many ways. They can be conceived, as Lawrence Levine does, as part of the history of human thought; as Alan Dundes considers them, as a source for insights into black family life as seen from the perspectives of members of the family; or, in Alex Haley's terms, as bits, pieces and patches of the past that form the oral history of a black family. Gladys Marie Frye considers them as one way enslaved blacks communicated the news of relatives separated from one another; and she considers the role of children in these storytelling sessions to be an aspect of black cultural history that has been too long overlooked.[9]

How *we* reacted to the stories, and how they were intended to function in my family, I deal with as the stories are told. The legends given here are, of course, written versions of oral traditions; I have written them down as they were taped or as I first remember hearing them. It is important to remember that they still circulate orally in innumerable versions and are never told in exactly the same way; the legends and the context in which they are transmitted are always changing. Unless otherwise indicated, the versions recorded here are the ones my mother Maggie told me.

During our formative years in Philadelphia, my mother Maggie told my brothers and me these stories whenever and wherever she pleased. She molded them to fit a given situation, refashioned them, placed upon them her own meanings and made them serve her purposes and our needs as she perceived them. Even those stories told to us as adults were designed to make the past applicable to the present.

Why have the stories and storytelling persisted in our family? The reason Maggie gave an outside researcher was simple: "It was good enough for Caddy, it was the way she taught Albert, it was good enough for Kate, it was the way she taught me, it was good enough for me, so I thought it was good enough for my children and I hope they will use storytelling to tell their children what they 'ought' to know about being human."[10]

When we were alone, she added another reason. She said, "Storytelling was good enough for Jesus, it is good enough for me."

Children of Strangers

The Gordon Family

All dates are approximate at the request of the family and because of the lack of precise data.

The First Generation   Caddy was born in 1833 or 1834, sold into slavery in 1842, and emancipated in 1863, when she was 29 years old. Caddy lived in Lynchburg, Virginia, from 1863 or 1864 until she died in 1919 at age 86.

The Second Generation   Albert and Kate were born about the same time, about 1860. They were emancipated at age three or four in 1863 or 1864. They married in 1883. Kate died in 1945, Albert in 1946.

The Third Generation   Rosebud, Prince, Adeline and Benny were born before the turn of the century. Rosebud and Adeline died in the early 1950s one week apart on the same day at the exact same time. Benny died mysteriously during the late '40s. Prince died in the '70s.

Maggie, William and Jimmie were born early in this century. They are the surviving members of the first three generations.

The Fourth Generation   Born to Maggie in the 1920s were Raphael (died in the War), Donald, Kathryn and Reginald.

The Fifth Generation   Born between the 1940s and 1970s were Donald's children, Ray, LaLee, Donald, Jr., Camilla, Marjorie, Bootsie, Sugie, Terry, Sidney, Kim, Adrienne and Tony; Kathryn's child, Susan; and Reginald's children, Lance, Renee and Sasha.

The Sixth Generation   Born in the 1970s were Ray's children, Tondhi and Johnathan; and LaLee's children, Danyelle and Dana.

The Gordon Family (1912).
From top to bottom and from left to right:
Benny   Prince
Rosebud   Adeline   Maggie
Kate   Albert   Caddy
     William   Jimmie

I
Caddy and Family
History

Caddy
(1912)

Introduction

Caddy was my maternal great-grandmother, and she was born free. A child of a stranger, she lived along with her brothers and sisters in a tiny house in Beaufort County about seven miles from Lynchburg, Virginia. Liza, her mother, was described as beautiful, black, with long hair that hung below her waist. She was part Cherokee, part African, and it is important to know that she was not mixed—with "white blood," but neither was she averse to white people.

Well, way back then in Beaufort County, nobody cared who mixed with whom—but the law. Nobody married. Liza didn't, she was no different from the rest. She was "kept" first by one Englishman, who died, leaving her with three children. Uncle Dave, Uncle Abraham and Aunt Laura they were called. They were white by nature, black by law, African and Cherokee by choice. They called themselves the "children of strangers." Then Liza was kept by another Englishman and she had a daughter by him. They called her Caroline, Caddy, the one we spoke of before.

When she was eight years old, Caddy was kidnapped and sold into the slave labor system. Liza sickened. She sat waiting, waiting for Caddy to return. Her other children of strangers left her. Dave called himself Carson—in other words, he gave himself a last name—and moved to Lynchburg, where he became the father of a son, referred to in these accounts as Cousin Dave. Abraham and Laura moved away, too, somewhere back up in the hills, over there in Beaufort County, Virginia.

Then one day Caddy returned. She brought with her her two children, children of strangers, Albert and Adeline. What was Albert like as a young man? Well, we know one thing, he had a last name. Caddy married a black man named Gordon. He was a gravedigger in the black graveyard, in Lynchburg. Caddy worked with her hands. She bought land. She had a "home house" (the first home of the Gordons) built. She put up with Mr. Gordon. But one day Mr. Gordon was caught making bootleg whiskey in the open graves and selling it to his regular customers—the live ones, that is—in broad daylight! Caddy got rid of Mr. Gordon. She kept only his name. And she and Albert worked as farmers.

By the time Albert was twelve he owned his own land, he owned a team of horses, a wagon, raised his own tobacco crop and "hawked it." Albert was raised in part by his Uncle Dave and the cousins, who called themselves the "bootmakers." And bootmakers they were, known to be the best bootmakers in the area. They were hard-riding, hard-loving, hard-living, tough-minded men, who wore "criers" in the boots they made. Whoever made the boots "cry" the loudest won the annual contest in bootmaking. Albert grew up and he was different from the rest. He was quiet, shy, and hardworking. He had a sense of humor but he was different from Caddy, yet totally unawed by her ability to dominate.

Then he met Kate. He fell in love. The bootmakers called a meeting. "Our 'cus' has found himself a woman. We have got to get together and make him the loudest crying boots in the land." Now Albert had never had criers in his boots. To him, boots were boots—not the measure of a man. But he succumbed to tradition, and the bootmakers put aside their contest that year. All concentrated on that single pair of boots. And they made Albert the loudest crying boots in the land, so they said. And Albert had a hard time getting those high-heeled boots on, much less learning to swing his feet and walk so those criers

Kate and Albert
(1940s)

would cry. But six of the bootmakers with the help of Albert finally got the boots on Albert's feet. Legend has it that it looked like the boots were going to make Albert cry before he could walk and make them cry. But he won. And they said that Kate heard Albert coming a mile away the first time he came calling. Ah, Kate had herself a man, couldn't she tell by the cry of his boots? And the bootmakers never let Albert forget that they helped him get a good woman, the woman called Kate, who was later to become the mother of Albert's seven children— Rosebud, Adeline, Prince, Benny, Jimmie, William and Maggie, my mother.

After Kate and Albert married, Caddy moved away, up the street a piece where she built her own home, and took care of Liza, until Liza died. And Caddy ate her breakfast and her supper every day with Kate and Albert. She was the great storyteller. Every evening after supper she would tell the children stories. Stories about people, about life, about living, about laughing.

The Gordons and Carsons were first and foremost Southerners. They brought with them wherever they went that black Southern tradition. The first generation were farmers, tobacco growers, factory workers, chairmakers and tradesmen. Most of the women stayed home and took care of the children. In my family they were all fundamental Baptists, attending church regularly, staying all day sometimes, then returning at night. They were independent people. Tough. Hunters and riders, engaging in races, community picnics, taking long walks in the country, picking blackberries, digging roots, making wine, canning, slaughtering hogs, and doing all things common to life in Lynchburg, Virginia, among blacks during Reconstruction.

They called their cousins "cus." They counted as kin their first, second, third, fourth and fifth cousins somewhat removed. Guns were standard equipment. The Gordons used guns primarily for hunting, and to protect themselves in the event anyone came hunting them. Death was not taken lightly, but life without dignity was death anyway, and life was more than a series of lessons in learning how to die. They had the gift of self-humor. And children had a place.

In the family it was Caroline, called Caddy, who started the tradition of oral storytelling using personal experiences. When she returned to Lynchburg during Reconstruction, she told Liza and her brothers what happened to her, and I know she told Albert and all the cousins. Caddy was the only one of Liza's children enslaved.

Caddy was a midwife, a farmer, a tradeswoman, a "wheeler and dealer." Most often she is simply described as "something else." But she was *the* storyteller. She suppressed nothing. But when she started to describe how it felt to be raped, Kate sent the children to bed. Caddy stressed family solidarity, self-respect, decency and dignity in her stories. All her stories were about people, there was no room for animal tales and other fictional lore.

When Rosebud and Adeline were teenagers around the turn of the century or thereabouts, when Maggie was small, Caddy brought them to Philadelphia, Pennsylvania, so they could find employment and make more money as "white." They lived for a short while with some cousins who were "passing" partially.[1] That is, they passed while they were at work and after work returned to a black neighborhood. They worked as white waitresses in downtown restaurants. But they did not like it. Anyway, it was against their principles, so they retired from the practice of "passing." So did the cousins. The cousins returned to Lynchburg, lived as blacks and never returned to Philadelphia.

Rosebud and Adeline stayed in Philadelphia. They worked as washerwomen and live-in domestics for rich white people. Rosebud took a course in hairdressing, bought a home in South Philadelphia in a black neighborhood and worked out of her home. She married first. Then Adeline married and her husband Ferdinand Nelson bought her a large home in North Philadelphia. He had a jitney business and Aunt Adeline took care of the books. So Rosebud and Adeline lived and died in Philadelphia. They always went "home" to Lynchburg, Virginia, whenever they could during the winter and every summer. That was a tradition in my family.

And then came the First World War. My uncles escaped for the most part the horrors perpetrated against black soldiers in the war. Prince, who was kicked in the head by a cow when he was young, was told he was going blind. When Caddy told him that there was nothing to do, she presented him with a fine white horse, told him to live life to the fullest and worry about going blind when the time came. This he proceeded to do, and was not a bit regretful that he was not drafted into a segregated army.

My uncles Jimmie and William were too young to be drafted. My uncle Benny enlisted in the Navy; when he returned to Lynchburg after the war, he had changed. He moved away from the house, where Kate and Albert lived. He did not live with Caddy. He did not live with Uncle Jimmie, Aunt Lillian or any of our cousins. He lived on the same street, in the house of a neighbor, where he rented a room.

Whether or not there were any stories about Uncle Benny I do not know. I know he had worked in a factory before the war; however, Benny never married. He never established a home for himself. He did not attend church. He always carried a shotgun in Lynchburg. He fell in love with a young woman he met on one of his visits north; they would meet and take pictures together. Uncle Benny was a private person during his lifetime and even died mysteriously, just before or during the 1940s. The young woman who loved him became a recluse. She never married.

Caddy continued to live in Lynchburg and make periodic trips to Philadelphia after the turn of the century. From Maggie, my mother, I learned that by the time Caddy had grown older, she had accumulated so much property "with her two hands" that she could afford to *give* it away.

She bought a large tract of land in Amos County, Virginia. A poor man, a sharecropper, made an agreement with Caddy. This agreement was oral. He would work the farm and take half of the crop profits. The agreement was never broken. They both did well. Caddy also gave the land for the new Baptist church in Lynchburg. When she heard they were having a drive to raise funds to buy land to build the church, she gave them the land. She was a religious woman, who rarely if ever went to church. However, Caddy was not an altruist—far from it. She never gave her children land. She made them *buy* it from her.

She was not a conformist by any means. She drank, she smoked, she chewed snuff. She cursed "in front of the children," much to the dismay of Kate and Albert, who were the most fundamental Baptists ever born, according to Maggie. To Albert and Kate, dancing, singing, having parties were "sinful." Not to Caddy. She laughed aloud, took Maggie and William to her house when they were growing up each Sunday morning and gave them what she called a "little toddy," which was, of course, diluted whiskey. There she told them stories. They in turned remembered their "grandma" as a storyteller and the woman who exerted a great influence on their lives. It is for this reason that most of the stories were told by and about Caddy and that the remembered incidents in Maggie's life seem to focus more on Caddy than on Albert and Kate.

My brothers Raphael, Donald and Reginald and I were born and raised in the 1920s and 1930s. By the time I was old enough to remember hearing these stories, we lived in a rented house in Philadelphia. The old stories are told the same way now as they were then. They were not meant to be modernized. A story may linger in the recesses of Maggie's memory and stay there until the situation triggers her memory and causes her to tell it.

Maggie is the major tradition-bearer in our family. She told me most of these legends before I was old enough to go to school. I have kept them alive by telling them to my daughter Susan, who in turn has told several of them to her younger cousins.

Stories

I cannot truthfully say that I remember the exact circumstances surrounding the first telling of the legends, as I have forgotten over the years. I know they were often repeated. They were usually told in the kitchen while my mother was preparing a meal or performing some other chore. She never sat to tell them and sometimes we would have to follow her from room to room to hear the end of a legend. They were never told as a series. I was the most avid listener, as I was the only girl and my mother, when she was exasperated with me, would say I was "Just like Caddy."

I never let her know that as far as I was concerned this was a most desired compliment. It was my life's ambition to be like Caddy when I was a little girl, as Caddy did all the daring things I secretly wanted to do. Frankly, Caddy comes to my rescue even now when some obstacle seems insurmountable to me. I cannot remember the first time I was told about Caddy being sold on the block when she was eight years old, but all during my childhood I remember having a sense of well-being in the knowledge that nobody could sell me.

Caddy—Version I

Caddy was only eight years old when she was sold on the block. After that she was always being sold. She was sent from plantation to plantation but she would always run away. She grew to be a beautiful young girl and that made the white women hate her. The white men loved her and sometimes she was taken to live in the big houses. Big houses or not, Caddy didn't want to be a slave. She would run away. When she was caught, she was usually hung in the barn and whipped across her naked back with a cat-o'-nine-tails. This didn't stop Caddy from running. She would run and she would be caught and she would be whipped. Do you think she'd cry when they whipped her with a cat-o'-nine-tails? Not Caddy. It would take more than a cat-o'-nine-tails to make Caddy cry in front of white trash.[2]

Susan reacted to this legend in a somewhat different manner than I did at her age, if I am to judge by her questions. She expressed concern that "Caddy wouldn't like her very much" because she has lots of white friends. She also asked what made people "trash." It never occurred to me to ask such a question, as I was already prejudiced against "white trash" before I knew what "white" was. When I was a child, we merely lumped all white people into two compartments—good and trash. It was very simple. Those who treated you decently were good. Those who did not were trash. Although I had white classmates, they were not my friends, as we were not closely involved with one another. We lived in separate worlds. Susan finally decided that she did not know any trash personally but had heard about "trash" from one of her white schoolmates while she was visiting her. It seemed that Ann, her friend, was going to allow Susan to play with a doll which was left at Ann's house until Ann realized that she had better not because her friend "didn't like coloreds." Susan assumed that Ann's friend was an example of "trash." She also encountered what she termed "trash" the first time she was chased and called a "dirty little nigger" by a woman who accused her of playing on her lawn. Susan came home full of glee to tell me how she took time to explain to the woman what a "nigger" really was and how she was "niggardly" not to let children play on her lawn. She wanted to know if it was all right to "sass" the woman the way she did since she was "trash." I told her she had handled the situation very well.

This is how Susan recorded me telling the story.

Caddy—Version II

Sometimes you think it would be nice to be a slave girl where you wouldn't have to be worried about financial problems and things. But when you hear this story I believe that it will change your mind. It's about a girl named Caddy. Caddy was my great-great-grandmother. She was only eight when she was sold on the slave block. After that she was always being sold. She had to be sent from plantation to plantation because she would always run away and sass the mistress. She would even sass people who weren't her mistresses. Well, she grew to be a beautiful young girl and that made all the white women hate her out of pure jealousy. The white masters loved her and sometimes she was taken into the big house to live. That didn't make any difference to Caddy. Big house, little house, great house, small house, it was all the same because they were just taking her in so that she would be more convenient for them. Sometimes she would run away so that she wouldn't be a convenient little handy hand, but was usually caught and then she was taken into the barn and hung up by her thumbs and whipped across her back with a cat-o'-nine-tails. It would hurt real bad but do you think Caddy would cry? Ah, you bet not! It would take more than a cat-o'-nine-tails to make Caddy cry in front of poor white trash. Maybe they were rich in money, but they were poor in brains. Caddy hated trash, black or white. Usually they had to sell Caddy because she was too hard to handle and would always be running away.

We found the legend of "What Caddy Did When She Heard That Lee Had Surrendered" the most delightful of all. We would ask our mother, who never said "bad" words unless they could be attributed to Caddy—who it was said "used vile language all the time"—to repeat the part where Caddy flipped up her dress over and over again. I would go to my room and practice flipping up my dress and saying "kiss my ass" in front of a mirror. As a teenager I remember how wonderful I thought it would be to be able to tell the whole white world to "kiss my ass." When Susan retold this legend for the tape recorder, she giggled and repeated the last line over and over.

What Caddy Did When She Heard That Lee Had Surrendered

Caddy had been sold to a man in Goodman, Mississippi. It was terrible to be sold in Mississippi. In fact, it was terrible to be sold anywhere. She had been put to work in the fields for running away again. She was hoeing a crop when she heard that General Lee had surrendered. Do you know who General Lee was? He was the man who was working for the South in the Civil War. When General Lee surrendered that meant that all the colored people were free! Caddy threw down that hoe, she marched herself up to the big house, then, she looked around and found the mistress. She went over to the mistress, she flipped up her dress and told the white woman to do something. She said it mean and ugly. This is what she said: "Kiss my ass!"[3]

I was taught to believe that my "aristocratic blood"—black and white—would help me overcome any insult or hardship I might encounter at the hands of "trash." This legend, while lessening somewhat the feelings of racial inferiority, did not erase them. In fact, there was a period in my life when I underwent intense internal conflict between feelings of inferiority and feelings of superiority. I never questioned the assumption that my African ancestors were kings and queens and my white ancestors were "quality" whites. I was often told, "they may be your color, but they're not your kind!" This reference, of course, was made to other blacks, assigned to the lowest stratum of the second-class citizenry, who seemed to reinforce the stereotypes in our own minds. It took me a very long time to realize that any profit gained from the mass of blacks would be a temporary and shameful profit. I now know that no person in America is safe as long as so many blacks are poverty-striken. When I related this legend to Susan I stressed responsibility rather than aristocracy.

How Caddy Found Her Mother

Caddy went out to find her mother in Virginia. She had two small children. They weren't by the same fathers but both the men were aristocrats, that means masters of fine plantations. Caddy was very proud of her children's blood. She used to always tell them, "There ain't no poor white blood running through your veins." Caddy told them that all the time. She told it to Albert and Adeline when they were little, and she told it to Kate when she became Albert's wife. That's one thing we can say with pride. There is no trash in our blood. It's good aristocratic blood. Caddy worked her way with those two children from Mississippi to Virginia. She was looking for her mother. She worked very hard because she aimed to make that aim. She met up with many troubles and hardships but she kept on. Then she found her mother. Aunt Liza was still living on a plantation but she was old and she was sick. Caddy took her to live with her and took care of her until she died. Caddy believed that you should take care of your family because your family are all that you have. Aunt Liza didn't die until she was ninety-two years old. That's a pretty old age as ages go. Caddy took care of her until the day she died. Caddy was a strong woman. Not in muscles but a strong woman in heart.[4]

The next legend stresses the need for respectability and character. These two qualities were indicative of the "better class." I venture to say that I was the most African-looking member of the family in several generations. Two of my brothers were blond with blue eyes and white skin; the other looked just like an Indian with silky black hair. All could "pass" for something other than black American. As a result my mother drilled Character, Respectability and Brains into me, to make up for my not being "good-looking." Good-looking according to the standards of the times meant being as white as possible, with hair as straight as possible and features as fine as possible.

I can remember hearing almost daily the saying, "it isn't what's on the outside that counts, it's what's on the inside," but I also remember being cautioned not to mention the fact that I had to have my hair straightened.

This is Susan's version.

Why Caddy Got Mr. Gordon Out of Jail—Version I

Caddy got married to a Mr. Gordon. Getting married in those days wasn't like getting married today. You know you didn't have all the frills, the long white dress, the blue dress, and the long cape, the big aisle with the music going "don don don don"— and the man with the vest and all that. Caddy never even bothered to go to a preacher. It was just enough for two people to want to be married. Anyway, Caddy wanted a last name for her children. Mr. Gordon was willing to give them his. That's how papa became Albert Gordon and Adeline, well, that's how she became Adeline Gordon [not the Adeline in the photographs, but a member of an earlier generation]. It's very important for children to have an honest last name. Now Mr. Gordon wasn't a very good man but he did have a last name and he did let Caddy have it for the children, so Caddy was willing to put up with his laziness and didn't say too much. You know, equal-equal. Finally, though, he left Caddy and got himself another "wife."

Caddy "got married" to a Mr. Rucker. Mr. Rucker was a very good man. Hard working and all that. But he died early. Caddy worked hard and saved her money. One day she heard that Mr. Gordon had gotten himself into some kind of trouble and was going to have to go to jail. You know what Caddy did? She went to the bank. And then she went to the courthouse. And then she went right up the middle aisle. She stood before the judge and then she reached down under her skirt and put the money on the table. She said, "Judge, I don't want no nigger with my children's name going to jail, so here I am to bail him out." Now everybody respected Caddy, even the judge, so he let Mr. Gordon go. Caddy was that kind of woman. Respectable. Caddy told Mr. Gordon that as long as her children had his last name she didn't want him laying around in any jail. Then she gave him some money and sent him home to his "wife." Caddy was like that. Respected. [5]

And this is the way I remember Maggie telling the story to me.

Why Caddy Got Mr. Gordon Out of Jail—Version II

Caddy got married to a Mr. Gordon. Getting married in those days wasn't like getting married today. Caddy never bothered to go to a preacher or anything. It was enough for two people to want to be married. Anyway, Caddy wanted a last name for her children and Mr. Gordon was willing to give them his. That's how papa became Albert Gordon and Adeline, Adeline Gordon. It's important for children to have an honest last name. Now Mr. Gordon was not a very good man, but he did have an honest last name and he let Caddy have it for the children. So Caddy put up with his laziness and didn't say too much. Finally though, he left Caddy and got himself another "wife." Caddy "got married" to a Mr. Rucker. Now Mr. Rucker was a good man, hard working and all but he died early. Caddy worked hard and saved her money. One day she heard that Mr. Gordon had gotten himself in some kind of trouble and was going to be sent to jail. Caddy went to the bank. She marched herself right up to the courthouse, marched right up the middle aisle. Stood before that judge. She reached down under her skirt and put the money on the table. She said, "Judge, I don't want no nigger with my children's name going to jail, so I'm here to bail him out." Now everybody respected Caddy, even the judge, so he let

Mr. Gordon go. Caddy was that kind of woman. Respectable. Caddy told Mr. Gordon that as long as he had her children's name she didn't want him laying around in jail. Then she gave him money and sent him home to his "wife." Caddy was like that. Respected.

About the age of four my brother Raphael became very ill and had to be hospitalized on and off for a period of fourteen years. This made money very scarce in our house and even with help from the other members of the family there were times when we ate by candlelight because the electricity had been cut off. As children it was difficult for us to understand why my mother took down the eviction notices as soon as the constable left. My mother always managed to put "good shoes on our feet and good food in our stomachs," and tell us how Caddy made her money and bought property in spite of adverse conditions. We sacrificed for years and I can never remember a time when we had enough money and weren't dodging the bill collectors, but we always felt it was worth it if "Ray C" could get better. He did. He was inducted into the army and died at nineteen in World War II. My mother was the first mother in the neighborhood to receive a gold star for her window and an American flag.

How Caddy Made Her Money and Bought Her Property

Caddy couldn't read or write but she sure could count money. She was never one penny short. Albert and Kate couldn't read or write either but Caddy taught them how to work hard and count money too. She said that there was only one way children could learn how to read and write. The grownups had to work hard and save the money. Caddy had all kinds of ways to make money. She was a midwife for the poor whites and Negroes. She would go around to all the restaurants and good houses on the other side of the tracks, pick out the spotted fruit that had been thrown in the garbage. Then she would come home, cut the

*spots off and make preserves and pies and go back and sell them
to the same folks who had thrown the fruit away!*

*She would come to Philadelphia about once a month and
buy up rag barrels which she had sent back home. Then she
would sort the rag barrels, and the clothes she could patch up
she would sell to the poor whites and to the Negroes. Then she
would make quilts out of rags and sell them too. That's how
Caddy made her money and bought her property.*

Every summer we went "home" to the South to visit Albert
and Kate. My uncle William would drive up from Lynchburg
and get us. My father never went with us and once I remember
asking him why. He replied that he "didn't want to get lynched."
I did not know what "lynched" meant, and since I loved going
south I could not understand my father's attitude. My mother
told me some years later that my father hated the South and
prided himself on "never having set foot below the Mason-
Dixon Line." My mother explained that he never went with us
because he was "hot-tempered" and was concerned that he
might do something to bring harm to us all if someone should
mistake my mother for a white woman married to a half-breed
"nigger." She then told me the following legend about how
Caddy brought the girls to Philadelphia. It was not until years
later that I could understand my father's insistence on remain-
ing in the North.

Why Caddy Brought the Girls
to Philadelphia

*Caddy couldn't read or write but she was truly a great woman.
She brought the whole family to Philadelphia on the excursions
when she came up to buy the rags sometimes. Kate couldn't
come because it made her sick to ride on the train. In fact, Kate
had to walk everywhere she went. Albert couldn't come very
often because he had to work. But Caddy would bring the children if they made good marks in school. They usually got good*

Rosebud and Adeline
(1912)

marks. *Kate would whip them every day for a week if they didn't. They couldn't linger after school to look in the store windows or anything. Kate and Albert were very strict like that.*

The children used to love to come to Philadelphia with Caddy because there they could "pass" and have fun. Caddy loved the trolley cars and the children used to ride all over the city with her. They had cousins who were "passing" and they stayed with their cousins. Caddy said that she and Cousin Dave had talked it over and they decided it was better to "pass" in the day and come home at night to a neighborhood that was colored. She said that way they wouldn't have to live with poor white trash. Living with poor white trash would be hell. Caddy said it was bad enough having to work with them all day but you could come home to your own people at night. She used to tell them terrible stories about people who passed over all the way and married white. She used to say they would come up with black nappy-haired babies and tell terrible things about what happened to them. She said you never can tell what's going to come out or pop up, so it's best not to take chances that way. Later when Rosebud and Adeline were grown, they came to Philadelphia to live with Cousin Dave and "passed" and got good jobs. Marjorie was still in school and Caddy would only bring her during vacation.

Since Marjorie was the youngest girl and William was the next-to-youngest boy, they were the ones who had to stay home and get ready to go to the seminary for colored students. They didn't really want to go to seminary. They wanted to come to Philadelphia and "pass." It sounded like so much fun. You see, they were never allowed to have fun in Kate and Albert's house. Kate and Albert were so strict that the only time the children had fun was when Caddy came over and did something terrible like use a lot of cuss words in front of Albert and Kate. Caddy had a vile tongue and Albert and Kate were trying to raise the children right. They didn't like Caddy to cuss. But they didn't

Cousin Dave Carson and Albert
(1940s)

say anything. Kate tried to say something about it once but it didn't work so she gave up.

During vacation Marjorie was glad to come to Philadelphia with Caddy. They would sit in the kitchen and wait for Cousin Dave and Rosebud and Adeline to come home and tell them what the whites would say about "niggers." Whites didn't know that they were colored. Caddy would be smoking her pipe. Sometimes she would laugh so hard she would almost swallow the smoke. She would spend hours telling them how to get even with the white trash that talked about "niggers." She knew some very terrible ways to get even too. She would tell them to Adeline and to Cousin Dave. Rosebud and Dave tried some of them but Adeline never would. Caddy used to tell her that the reason she was so simple was because she thought she was white for sure. She used to warn Adeline that she was in for a rude awakening. She really did like Adeline a lot though. She just didn't want her to get hurt because she was so soft. Caddy used to say that there was nothing more cowardly than "trash." Especially white trash. That is why they have to talk so big and act so ugly. Caddy couldn't stand colored people who simpered around white folks either. She said the best thing to do is mind your business, don't linger, don't talk, don't believe and never act afraid no matter how scared you really are. Caddy said you could only die once. Better die for something than nothing. You have to fight every inch of the way to be free, every inch of the way to be free.

My Uncle William finally came to Philadelphia to live with us and I could not understand why he insisted I learn how to fight, when my mother was trying so hard to make me into a "little lady." I remember going into the cellar with Uncle Bill, my brothers and my father for boxing lessons, but I cannot remember ever having to defend myself physically. After my mother told us the following two legends, "How Caddy Taught William Not To Be a Coward" and "How Caddy Made Marjorie

Adeline
(1911)

Find a Way To Walk Over the Bridge," I could understand my
Uncle William a little better. Recently I asked my brother Donald, who is a marvelous storyteller with a keen sense of humor
and a vivid imagination, what these legends meant to him. He
recalled that the only time he found it a little unhandy to "stand
up and fight" was when the Germans caught him squatting on a
makeshift john in France during World War II.

How Caddy Taught William
Not To Be a Coward

*William had to walk by the poor white section one day by him-
self because he was late coming home from school. Some
"trash" boys saw him and he saw them and he got scared and
they chased him all the way home. Caddy and Kate were in
Kate's kitchen when he ran in puffing for breath. Kate asked
him what was wrong and he told her what happened. Kate beat
him for running. Then Caddy beat him again. Caddy told him
if he ever ran away from "trash" again she was going to beat his
ass every day and that's what happened. William would run and
Caddy would beat him—every day for about a week. Poor
William. The other children used to cry because he got so
many beatings. Then Kate would beat them so they wouldn't be
wasting good tears for nothing.*

*Finally William caught one of the white trash and beat him
almost to death. When he came home that day he wasn't out of
breath and he didn't look scared any more. Caddy and Kate told
him he had done the right thing and Kate gave him an extra
piece of hoe cake which he loved. Then Caddy went to get the
shotguns. She and Kate took turns sitting at the window with
the shotguns all that day and all night. Kate was meaner than
Caddy and she would have blown somebody's head off for sure.
Albert went to bed with his shotgun because he had to get up
and go to work in the morning. Caddy sent for all the boy cousins. Cousin Dave's younger children and all the children had
to walk back and forth from school together for a long time.*

Nothing happened but Kate and Caddy sat up a whole week all night and all day taking turns—just in case. Kate said nothing happened because we were respected and Caddy said it didn't hurt to be respected by high and low alike.[6]

How Caddy Made Marjorie Find a Way
To Walk Over the Bridge

Marjorie had to walk over the bridge every day to get to school and every day she would meet this "trash" boy who would make her get off the bridge and walk in the street where the horses walked. She did this every day. He would wait for her on the bridge and when she got ready to walk across he would push her off into the street. Caddy found out what was happening. I don't know who told her but she called Marjorie in the kitchen and she said "Maggie, you will have to find a way to walk on the bridge. You are just as white as the 'trash' that pushed you off of the bridge and if the bridge is for whites they can't push you off because you are just as white as they are. It's up to you to find your own way to walk across the bridge."

Now when Caddy told you you had to find your own way, you had better find it. Marjorie went to her room to think up a way. The only way she could think of was her mama's old rusty hatpin. She put it in her handbag the next day so nobody would see it and she went off to school as usual. Sure enough after school there he was waiting on the bridge, and when he went to push her she took the hatpin and stuck it clean through his arm. Then she ran home and told Caddy what she had done. Well, Caddy said she had found a way but it was the wrong way, but she wouldn't let anybody bother Marjorie because she had told her to find a way and Marjorie had found the only way she could. Years later Marjorie's brother Benny was working in a factory and a foreman came up to him and asked him if he had a sister. He said, "Yes." Caddy always taught the children not to say "Yas suh, No suh" and "Yas 'um and No mum" to white folks. The foreman said, "Is her name Maggie?" Marjorie's

brother said "yes." The foreman pulled up his sleeve and showed
him a deep scar on his arm. Then he said to him, "I almost lost
an arm because of Maggie, but you know one thing? She was
right."

The most recent Caddy legend I heard was told to me by my
mother several years ago while we were waiting in line at the
supermarket. It seemed to strengthen my belief that Caddy has
really left us rich in the ability to laugh, to perceive, to struggle,
and strive for wisdom.

As told to me, this legend had no title; Marjorie started to talk
about Caddy as we sometimes do when we have a bit of time.

Untitled

You know Caddy was a midwife for the poor whites and Negroes
and she had to go from house to house to deliver babies. Many
times she tended the other sick people while she was in the
house. One day she came home cussing and fussing because
somebody had put a diaper on an old man who was not able to
control his bladder. Caddy said, "You work hard all your life so
you can get a bed of your own, then, when you get old, some-
body straps you up so you can't even piss on it."

Marjorie and I laughed so loud we attracted attention and had
to remember where we were. I imagine people wondered what
the white woman with her black friend found so hilarious!

Every so often I somehow manage to delude myself into be-
lieving that I am superior to the mass of black humanity because
of some superficial individual achievement. Whenever this
happens I try to remember the following legend and stumble
back to reality.

Don't Forget How It Was To Be a Slave

Caddy suffered a lot. She suffered most all of her life, but she
was a fighter. That's what she taught the children to be—fight-
ers. You know, one day she was peeling apples in a big house

and the mistress said something to her and she sassed the woman back. The mistress took the knife and cut Caddy's arm straight through to the bone and Caddy didn't have anybody to help take care of it or anything, so she just keep rubbing salt into it until it got well. She used to show the children the marks on her back from the cat-o'-nine-tails. They were thumb deep, but she didn't want them to forget what slavery was like.

The last time Marjorie saw Caddy she was running for the trolley. She was trying to make a train home. She was eighty-six and she said she "was a little bit tired," just a "little bit tired." She died about a week later. Before she died she took time to tell Kate to get her in the ground quick. She said to Kate, "Kate, don't let a lot of niggers pray and speak in the 'unknown tongue' over me." You know, next to "trash" Caddy hated preachers and church-going hypocrites more than anything in this world and she let everybody know it including the church-going hypocrites and the preachers. Nobody questioned Kate either, they knew better than to do that. Kate never talked much and she never cried, not even when Caddy died. But nobody questioned Kate. She just buried Caddy with no praying and that was that.

To say that internal conflict, race hatred and contempt were destroyed by these stories would be untrue. They served the purpose of diminishing feelings of racial inferiority imposed upon us as children. I know that missing here is much wisdom learned and transmitted by other blacks to their descendants, for I am sure that Caddy had many counterparts throughout the land.

II
Our Childhood

Aunt Adeline and Kathryn (the author)
(1930)

Introduction

When we were children (this was around 1930), we lived in a large rented house in North Philadelphia, full of the smell of baking bread, beans, fried potatoes and onions.

We smelled the famous "goose grease" used for aches and pains. We ran wild and fought each other furiously, but we sometimes *managed* to behave well in school.

School was dreadful. We sat. Our hands were folded. We heard that George Washington never told a lie, that the Indians were savages, that the cowboys and the Puritans and the people who settled this dear land had really done the Indians a great favor. Africa? What was that? Slaves were happy, because they were brought here to be civilized.

But when school was over, we could go home, home to Maggie, our mother, who told us her stories, too.

And we visited our Aunt Adeline and our Aunt Rosebud, who were like surrogate mothers. They had no children of their own. Aunt Rosebud had a little dog, she loved that little dog. She named him "Ming Toy." She took that dog everywhere but to church. That dog, to me, was a damn nuisance, but of course I couldn't say damn, because Maggie did not allow bad language. She and Kate are the reasons these stories are so clean. They suppressed everything connected with sex, and other "nasty" subjects.

Cursing and references to personal business were not allowed in our house. So we cursed, naturally, out in the street, to impress our peers with our sophistication.

In a few years we moved to another large rented house near Germantown in a changing neighborhood, mostly black Southern migrants. Educated people, they read the *New York Times,* like my father, Raphael Lawson. They were nationalistic like my father. But *God* was the head of the household—Maggie said so and she was the mother in our house. All she did was take care of us. She had her hands full.

Maggie had a code of "don'ts" that read like the *Egyptian Negative Confessions.* "Don't forget to wash your underwear, because if you forget, you *know* what is going to happen to you tomorrow on your way to school? You are going to be run down by a *garbage truck* and taken to the hospital. And there you will be, surrounded by strangers all dressed in white. Staring down at you, stretched out, with that dirty underwear stinking. Do you think I'm coming down and claim you as my child? No, indeed." So naturally we would take a chance.

But Maggie loved to dance, particularly the Charleston, and she taught us how to do the Charleston, and how to run and hide in the cellar if the bell rang in the daytime. Nobody in our neighborhood rang the doorbell in the daytime but bill collectors. Everybody else knew the door was open. Everybody left the door open in those days. So, when the doorbell rang it was the signal. Cellar time. Down we went. Giggling and stumbling around in the dark, trying not to cough as the dust crawled up in our throats choking us and stifling our giggles. Maggie was right there with us, wondering out loud how long that damn, and she would say damn, bill collector was going to lean on the bell pestering poor people when they were obviously not at home. Then once the crisis was over, Maggie would remind us not to lie because she could smell a liar. A liar was also a thief.

I don't know exactly when our cellar sessions came to a halt. It seemed that one day Maggie was afraid that my Aunt Rosebud, who had a car by that time, would drop by, and since my Aunt Adeline was living with my Aunt Rosebud, what would they think of the Gordon descendants teaching their children to

Donald and R. C.
(1930)

hide in cellars? Worse—suppose my *father* came home and found his wife and children crouched in the cellar hiding from a bill collector. Especially when he had given her the money to pay the bill and she had used it to take us to the circus. The side show Maggie loved—and the zoo! And when she spent the bill money she said that was our "secret."

But this particular day, now remember, I don't know who it was that Maggie sent to the door. But since my brother Raphael was in the hospital most of the time, it had to be my brother Donald, my brother Reginald or me. Whoever it was, Maggie told the one who was supposed to go to the door, to open the door, say to the bill collector, "my mother is not at home," then slam the door and run back to the kitchen.

So, one of us went to the door and said "my mother said to say she is not at home." But before the door could be shut, the bill collector said, "Ask your mother when *will* she be home." Now the "dum dum" who answered the door stood in the door-way and yelled back to Maggie, "Hey mama, the man wants to know when *will* you be home?" And Maggie yelled back, "tell that fool that I'll be home when I *damn please, that's when* I'll be home."

Well, we stopped running to the cellar. Maggie faced the fact that we were growing up. She could no longer fool us and make a lie look like a "secret" or tell us to respect ourselves and our dignity while we were crouching in the cellar hiding.

At the same time, we lived among Philadelphia's finest, join-ing in the little exclusive clubs for black children. Dressing up in our finery and walking down to Rittenhouse Square. Joining the Easter Parade. With mary jane shoes, clean underwear, beautiful clothes, manners. Spick-and-span, enough to make any mother's heart pound with pride.

And we learned to rise to our feet in the presence of our el-ders. My brothers learned to pull out chairs and open doors for ladies. We learned to keep quiet and to be charming when

Aunt Adeline,
Aunt Rosebud holding Ming Toy,
and Maggie (1938)

grown folks were talking, and not to have big ears and big mouths and put the family business in the street.

And we learned how to develop self-discipline. To thank God for his blessings and to remember that Maggie knew our tricks, that she was not born old.

My father taught us how to read the *New York Times*—from cover to cover, including the stock market reports and the obituary columns. So we learned to hate the *New York Times*, especially on Sunday.

Sunday was also the time when our Aunt Rosebud, dressed in her church clothes, did her duty and came by to take us for a ride at ten miles an hour. We would stop at the rusty trolley car tracks and Aunt Rosebud with "Ming Toy" in her arms would get out, adjust her fur piece, look up and down the tracks for trolleys, get back in the car, and proceed to the insane asylum.

Aunt Rosebud and Aunt Adeline, who was sweet, gentle and kind, would let us get out of the car and look through the bars while they went to get my Uncle Ferdinand. Uncle Ferdinand was my Aunt Adeline's husband. He was a fine-looking man. He graduated from Bucknell College and finished law school. His mother died in an insane asylum, so he and Aunt Adeline had decided they would marry but have no children. And when Uncle Ferdinand lost all his money, he went quietly mad.

We would wave to Uncle Ferdinand, but he did not know us, not even me and I knew he loved me better than the rest of them, other than Aunt Adeline. But Aunt Adeline would wave and make motions for us to wave, and she would smile and it would go on like that. They always took Uncle Ferdinand a box of good food, Southern cakes and things. He would sit and look blank. Then Aunt Adeline and Aunt Rosebud would come back to the car, and Aunt Rosebud would say, "Don't cry Addie, Nelson feels no pain."

Then it would be summer in Lynchburg again. Running barefooted, remembering not to "mess over" Kate. Listening to Uncle Benny home from his job at the factory explain why this country belongs to the people Columbus found when he got here. The sound of the voices of the multitude of cousins. "Here comes our little brown-skinned 'dum dum' cus from the *North*," said my blond, blue-eyed cousin, a Carson, sweezing me with strong white arms.

We had a black cousin Lucy and a white cousin Lucy. Our black cousin Lucy lived in a white neighborhood in Philadelphia, and was a caterer, a successful one. Our white cousin Lucy lived in Lynchburg, in the section where all the black folks lived. She was a housewife, she was married to Cousin Dave Carson, and they had children our age. And we would listen to Uncle Jimmie sitting on the porch next door, grinning, telling stories, laughing, Aunt Lillian, his wife, saying with a long Southern drawl, "All right now, Jimmie, I think it's time you stopped now—ain't nobody laughing no more but you."

Lynchburg was going to Uncle Prince's house, drinking homemade root beer. Staring at the dent in his forehead, remembering that one day he would go blind because when he was taken out of school he had to milk cows and one kicked him in the head. What did it feel like to be kicked in the head by a cow and live all your life knowing you are going blind? Well, since there is nothing to be done about it, it is better to live, marry, own a pool hall, have a nice house, with a wife who can make the best homemade root beer in the world.

Uncle William was the one who always came back to Philadelphia with a little something for Addie. Addie was sick. So they all would come, by train, by car, one by one, the Gordons. Aunt Adeline was still sick when I went away to college. She sent me a dollar a week; in a scribbled, wobbly handwriting the letter read, "With love, from your Aunt Adeline." I, at last, was grown.

One of the most commonly shared experiences among blacks of my generation as children was obedience. By obedience I do not mean obedience only to one's parents, rather every older adult was a medium of social control—and we were hard to control. We did not sit and listen to old Uncle Remus tell stories about tricky rabbits. As a child, I never remember hearing such a story at home, nor do I remember ever *sitting down*, listening to my mother tell family stories, unless I was eavesdropping.

However, I do remember one incident because it brought about a great change in my life. It is connected with a story in which Maggie mentions casually that when she was young she was scared to death of Baptists because they "hollered and shouted so much." She also confessed that since the whole Gordon family were Baptists she could "hardly wait" to get to Philadelphia to "get rid of having to go to the Baptist church."

This confession was a mistake. Maggie was sending my brother Donald and me to the Episcopalian church in our neighborhood, each and every Sunday.

One Sunday morning as we were getting ready to go to church, my brother Donald asked my mother an innocent question: "Mama, is it true what you said about God being everywhere, even in the toilet and that He would answer your prayers even in the toilet if you were sincere?" My mother said, "Yes." (It was a detail she put into practically every story she told.) My brother replied, "Well, I would much rather go in the toilet and talk to God, because I am too scared to go to church with all those Baptists hollering and shouting so much." (Donald thought we were going to a Baptist church.) My mother sent my brother to the bathroom and sent me on to church. I sat in church wondering what I could do to keep from going to church again. When I returned home, I told my mother that the Episcopalians made me jump up and down so much my legs and feet ached. She rubbed them with goose grease and sent me to bed for the rest of the day.

My mother still tells this story and still mentions the Baptists, but she modifies her remarks to fit the sensibilities of the members of the family who happen to be Baptists. However, my brother Donald still remembers this story. He says it is the best thing that ever happened to him in his life. To know that God was omnipresent and available for consultation in the toilet meant we never had to go to church again, nor did my mother have to apologize for sending us and staying home herself.

If my mother and I were "walking down the avenue" on a Saturday night and I saw something I wanted and could not afford, she would invariably tell me a story about her own childhood that would be so terrible that it was obviously designed to make me ashamed of my selfishness. I would not persist.

Or we would be sitting in the kitchen at supper time, looking askance at a plate full of fried potatoes and onions but no meat. My mother would sense our dissatisfaction. Invariably, she would tell us the story of how my grandfather Albert had to walk all the way from Mississippi to Virginia at the age of three, ending with, "What do you think he would have given for a nice plate of hot fried potatoes and hot biscuits?" There was no such thing as the "good old days" when my mother was a child. There was no such thing as the "good old days" for black folks, period.

Sometimes we knew we were "in for" stories. Maggie would stand on the porch waiting on report card day. We would run to escape her and the stories. My brother Donald and I used to flunk "conduct." Flunking "conduct" in school was a deadly sin in our house. It was then we heard stories about how much our ancestors had sacrificed just so we could go to school. They spent their whole lives making painful X's on banknotes so we could go to school and flunk "conduct." Then came the stories of unappreciative children whose mothers sacrificed to send them to school. Then when they received their education, they were *ashamed* of their ignorant mothers! This to me was so great a tragedy that I *stayed* in school. But Donald *quit* school as soon as possible. He wanted to be an artist. He said he did not want to go to college and he did not go. He could not make a living at his artistry, so he worked as a bartender, a cook, and at many other jobs to support his twelve children and his wives. Yet he always kept in touch with his artistic desires and paints classical style whenever he has time. My brother Reginald also did not want to go to college. He wanted to become a jeweler.

He did not need a college education for that, he needed an apprenticeship.

I did not go to college *because* my ancestors sacrificed so I could go—I went to college to get away from home. I wished with all my soul that Caddy had been with me there so I could have read to her the words of the authorities on slavery who never had an enslaved ancestor and never talked to an ex-slave or a descendant of one. I laugh at my own foolishness, too. This foolishness includes academic insistence on what "ought" to be, whether or not it is. I, for one, have no idea who put the term "merely," in front of "anecdotal," or who proclaimed that entertainment and education were deadly enemies. Our family folklore, especially the stories told to us by Maggie in the third part, were told for the specific purpose of making us laugh at the absurdity of "color" and "race" and the nonsense that clutters up the minds of many people around the world today.

These stories did allow my mother to inform us of what *she* thought we "ought" to know, whether we liked it or not, whether we accepted it or not. In addition, I am convinced that my mother fashioned these stories to function to serve her own needs. Many times I have heard her say, particularly when we, as teen-agers, sneered at storytelling, "Well, I have tried to raise you right. I have tried to live my life each day, knowing I have done my best not to hurt or harm another living soul. I have tried to raise you right and to tell you the things you ought to know. I know I say things you don't want to hear about yourself, but who is better to tell you than your own mother? I know you don't want to hear it sometimes because you know it is the truth. But I have to tell you so I can go to bed at night and get a good night's sleep."

My mother does live her life the way she describes it. But written down it seems as though she is apologizing to us. Nothing could be further from the truth. Maggie may not have hurt another living soul, but she would never allow herself to be pushed around by anyone, especially us.

Stories

One of the oldest legends in our family is the story of "How Aunt Rosebud Got Her Name." The children of my generation were not told the complete story until we were old enough to understand it. The legend was refashioned to fit our sensibilities as we were growing up. We were taught to value our Aunt Rosebud as a very special Gordon. She was the first child *born* with the Gordon last name. While her exact age was never revealed, it may be assumed that she was born during the Reconstruction era. Evidently, earlier the legend was used to shape the attitudes of the younger Gordon children toward their older sister, Rosebud, and to shape Rosebud's perception of herself. When we were finally told the entire story, the point was stressed that it was no accident that Aunt Rosebud was the only Gordon child named after a flower.

The story of "How Aunt Rosebud Got Her Name" has existed as part of our family legends for more than seventy-five years.

How Aunt Rosebud Got Her Name

You know how Caddy used to sell things to the poor whites and to the other white folks. Those that lived on the other side of town. Well, everybody respected Caddy, and she used to tell them what to do and all when they got sick or the doctor couldn't do anything for them. Well, one day Caddy was at the back door selling these folks something, I don't remember what it was, and she saw this young girl in the back yard hanging up clothes. So this was Kate, and Caddy found out that Kate had been raised up by these folks, they were good Christian folks, and they had raised Kate ever since she had been a baby. Well, anyway, they arranged for Kate to marry when she was old enough and Kate moved away with her husband. It was not long after they were married when her husband was killed at work. I think he was electrocuted or something like that. Anyway, Kate was pregnant and he didn't have no folks and she didn't either. So she went back to the white folks who had raised her and they took her in.

You know they had raised Kate to be a lady, so you know we never heard Mama talk loud or even laugh out loud. She would smile, and she was a good cook and all. Well, anyway, Caddy got to know Kate pretty well and she told Kate about her son Albert. And she asked Kate would it be all right if she could get the white folks' permission to have Albert come call on Kate. And the white folks said that it was all right, that Albert could call on Kate.

So Albert and Kate would always sit in the backyard. And they always sat near the rose bushes, where the buds were, because they didn't have anything to talk about at first, you know, so they would always talk about the rose bushes and the rosebuds, how beautiful were the rosebuds.

So finally one day Albert reached up and picked a rosebud and asked Kate to marry him. He promised to take care of her child, even if it was a child of a stranger. He said Caddy was the child of a stranger, and that he was a child of a stranger, and that Kate was the child of a stranger, but that when she married him she would become one of the Gordons. He said the children of strangers deserved to be loved, and he believed he would take care of Kate and her child just like Caddy took care of him. And he asked Kate if the baby was a girl could they name her Rosebud. They could love little Rosebud who would be called Rosebud Gordon, she would be a Gordon, because Kate would be a Gordon, because he was a Gordon.

So Kate and Albert were married by law, and Kate went to

Rosebud
(1912)

live in Caddy's house with Albert. When the baby was born she was a girl and they named her Rosebud. And Caddy built her own house and sold the home house to Papa and Mama. And Papa was a good man and we loved him sometimes better than we loved Mama and Caddy because he was always willing to listen to us and sneak us candy and sweets down in the back house after he came home from work. He loved every one of us, but he always seemed to love Rosebud the most. She was something special to him, he always called her "Papa's little rosebud" and she was told she was a child of a stranger just like Albert and like Caddy and Kate. And Papa taught us to call her "Sister" and taught us that in the Gordon family children of strangers deserved to be loved. Kate was always telling me that I loved my children too much; I guess I do, but one thing I know, I couldn't have a better sister than "Rosebud." "Sister" was always good to me. [1]

The legend of "The Whipping and the Promise" is as old as or older than the story of "How Aunt Rosebud Got Her Name." It describes a ritual in child-rearing practices that has now been abandoned. However, the legend describing the ritual is crucial; it provided us with concrete knowledge of what we had escaped *from.* Although Maggie whipped hard, she constantly reminded us that *anything* was better than the whipping *and* the promise.

The Whipping and the Promise

When we were little Caddy used to give us what we called a "whipping and a promise." This had nothing to do with the "lick and the promise" where you smack the children and promise that if you have to do it again, you will give them another little tap. If we were caught doing something we weren't supposed to, she would send us out back to get some switches off the trees. We would have to get those green switches, the kind that wouldn't break. And she would make us take down our drawers and the boys would have to take down their pants. She said she didn't believe in whipping clothes, so she would whip us on our naked behinds. And she whipped, too. And all the while she was whipping, she was telling us why she was whipping so hard. She said she didn't believe in whipping easy because we might forget it. The worst part though was the promise. I never will forget the promise part, because that was the worst part. See, she would whip us, then she would promise us another whipping the next week for the same thing. And she made us promise to remind her that she owed us a whipping. Well, we were scared not to remind her because if she remembered, well it wasn't no telling what she would do because we broke a promise. I think the worrying was worse than the whipping because you had to think about how it wasn't over, you know. How you were going to get it again the next week. And she would whip us just as hard the second time as she did the first time. Caddy was good to us but in those days children didn't get away with what they do now, they [parents] had all kinds of ways to make you mind.

I still don't believe in that promise thing though, because children shouldn't have to worry about whippings. Just whip them and let it go at that, but whip them hard enough and they will remember.[2]

In "The Whipping and the Promise" we learned that children are not passive spectators to parental rules and regulations. They may rebel outright and attempt to break the rules, and suffer the consequences, or they may abandon as parents a form of discipline they feel was too harsh. Any honest analysis of the function of our family legends involves the examination of constancy and change, and, most important, the reality of conflict among family members. This was particularly significant for us in the case of conflict between the two venerated authorities, Caddy and Kate.

We were taught that in most things Caddy and Kate were staunch allies. Rarely did they disagree. Even more rare were frank and open discussions of their differences in front of the Gordon children. Perhaps this is why the following legend, which I have titled, "Caddy, Kate and All God's Children," still enjoys wide currency among individual family members today. I am firmly convinced that both Caddy and Kate were aware that they were dealing with a fundamental issue that would exert a tremendous influence on the lives and attitudes of succeeding generations. They were consciously or unconsciously recruiting allies. I know when Maggie told us about this conflict she did so for the very same reason.

Caddy, Kate and All God's Children

She [Caddy] used to come for supper with us, and after supper she would tell us her stories about slavery. These were stories about things she had seen done to other people and things she had done to her. I used to cry when I heard her talk about slavery. I thought Caddy had been everywhere in the world. Kate would listen while Caddy told us these stories because she had never been out of Lynchburg. She couldn't ride on anything; it made her sick. So she hadn't been anywhere that she couldn't walk. She didn't remember slavery because she was born a slave but she was only about three years old when slavery was over. Caddy was like a mother to Kate in a way, but Kate had her own mind. I don't think Caddy would have respected her if she didn't.

Kate taught us that everybody was a child of God, even all white people. Caddy said that was a "damn lie," that if Kate had lived with some of those poor white trash during slavery she wouldn't be so anxious to teach her children to love white folks. The only time I remember Kate and Caddy really fussing was one night in the kitchen when I was small, when Caddy told us we should hate poor white trash. Kate said for Caddy to teach us how to hate was to make us form a cancer on our souls. I remember how Caddy told Kate that that was the most stupid thing she ever said, "to try to teach my [Caddy's] grandchildren to love the poor white trash like those who put these whip marks on my back."

Then Caddy would strip down to the waist and show us her back. It was awful, there wasn't a space left without a mark on it. It was awful. Caddy said that God didn't have a damn thing to do with slavery. Nothing. That all those poor white trash were the devil's children. She taught us a lot of things like that about the devil's children. She said the devil put more children on earth than God did. And she taught us that nobody respects a slave, not even the slave's own children. Mama was a good woman; Caddy was too, but she did not believe in loving all white people because they were God's children. Caddy said she didn't hate all white folks, or love them either. She respected those who respected her. But she said she would hate poor white trash till the day she died.

Well, I don't believe in hate. I think you can dislike somebody's behavior, but hate is poison, you poison yourself with hate. Kate said that hate formed a cancer on the soul. In that way she was different from Caddy, but I loved them both. But I believed Kate. I always believed in God, ever since I was a child. I just didn't like the Baptists when I was little, that's all. They used to sing and holler and shout and talk in tongues and all that stuff, and scare me to death when I was a child. And Mama would sit there just as quiet as she could be. I used to wish I could hurry and grow so I could go to Philadelphia just to get rid of the Baptists. Mama and Papa were Baptist; they were as strict as they could be. When we got a piano Papa wouldn't even let us open it on Sundays unless we better be going to play a hymn. [3]

When I first heard the story of the conflict between Caddy and Kate, I immediately sided with Caddy. I remember my confusion. How could Kate and Maggie teach us to love poor white trash? How could we fight without hate? Caddy's philosophy made more sense to me at the time. In all fairness to Kate and Maggie, even if Caddy had been totally irrational, it would have made no difference to me. I did not want to imagine Caddy as a "loser." I loved Caddy *because* she was often pictured as a "hell-cat." If she had been godlike and saintly she would have lost me, because even as a young child I knew I was far from being the "little lady" that Maggie tried so hard to make me become.

I did not understand until much later what Maggie meant when she said, "If they can make you hate them, they *got you!*" By the time I was a teenager I was convinced that if I had a soul, I was destined to die with a diseased one.

My brother Donald's oldest daughter, Ray, was raised by Maggie. When she heard this legend she pledged allegiance to Maggie and Kate. I told this legend to Susan when she was about ten years old. She asked, "Who made God?" When I admitted I did not know, she thought about the story. Then she said, "Well, Mother, I still have a lot of wonderment in me." To me, this seemed the classic answer to the question of how these stories functioned: they kept alive in us the spirit of "wonderment."

At the other end of the spectrum were what I call the "comfort and challenge" stories. Both Caddy and Kate, stern disciplinarians though they were, were not addicted to thinking that whippings provided the solution to all the problems encountered in raising children. They firmly believed in the gift of "ownership" and independence. The next legend is typical of the "comfort and challenge" stories transmitted to us over the years.

The Bed

They say we had a cousin, a boy who used to wet the bed every night. You know Kate was a wise woman and she had her own way of doing things. She was able to do something about this boy. You know what she did? She told this boy, a little thing now, a little boy. She told him to come to her house, and he did. She took out some money and told him that she was going to give him that money so he could buy himself a bed. Can you imagine that? She said since the bed would be his he could do whatever he wanted to with it. If he wanted to piss all over it nobody could punish him because he owned the bed. You know, she even took that little child and let him pick out his own bed! They said that boy never wet the bed again.[4]

Kate was a wise and patient woman but she was far from perfect or predictable. The next legend is one of a kind; it revealed to us a part of Kate that was rarely exposed. It happened one day when William did not go to school. This meant that Maggie had to walk through the white section of town alone. Maggie told us that on her way home she stopped "only a minute or two" to look at a doll displayed in a store window. She claims she was "two minutes late" arriving home. For us this story served another function as we grew older; it helped explain that when Maggie insisted that we be home at a certain time, she meant *exactly* on time or ahead of time. For example, if she told us to be home at nine o'clock, and we were one minute late, we would be punished. Her rationalization for the punishment was worry. She would say something like this: "If you could be home at one minute *after* nine you could have been home at nine. One minute of unnecessary worry is one minute too much for me." In addition, this story contained within it a warning. It warned us not to try to "mess over" Kate on our summer visits to Lynchburg. We did not. For we remembered that Maggie had warned us that Kate was silent, dangerous and still, like deep water that drowns.

The Doll, the Flat Iron and the Bee

I remember once Kate almost killed me. Well, she would have if I hadn't ducked. I was late coming home from school and when I walked in the kitchen she was ironing. Those days it was those flatirons they used. And she just took the flatiron and threw it at me without letting me open my mouth. I ran outside. I was scared to go back in the house but I couldn't get in any way but the kitchen; I had to go back in. And when I went back in she just kept on ironing and didn't say a word. I went on upstairs. But later at supper time I went on down with the others and I didn't tell a soul, not even William. Well, Caddy and Kate were in the kitchen cooking and Albert was there and we all sat and ate like we always did. Kate acted like nothing had happened and she didn't even tell anybody that I had been late coming home from school, because everybody knew that a whipping and a promise and worse was for that. But I was never late again.

One day I thought I was going to be late and I started running. I stepped on a bee and it stung me. We didn't wear shoes to school in the springtime, and I was crying to beat the band, but I got in the kitchen on time. Kate said, "What's wrong with you, Maggie?" and I told her a bee had stung me on my foot. So she told me to sit down and stop crying, to think about what I did to the poor bee. But she was putting something, I don't know what it was, on my foot. Soon it stopped hurting but I kept remembering afterward that if a bee stings you it dies. Anyway, that's what we were taught. Well, we hated some things they did, Kate and Caddy I mean, but they did it for our own good and they had a lot of troubles in the South raising children.

In another legend about Kate we learned to value silence and not to fear it.

Kate and the Educated Ladies

Mama used to belong to a church social group, you know. It was a ladies' group and all the ladies were better educated than Mama was. They could read and write and talk about a lot of things that Mama didn't know anything about. But Mama used to go to each and every meeting. She wore a big hat with flowers on it, and she would come back and tell us everything that happened at the church. You know, Caddy and Kate were very religious people. Everything Caddy got she got with her two hands [Maggie used to make a gesture at this point, holding out her two hands palms up]. Think of that, all that property and everything with her two hands. You know when they got ready to build a church, you know Caddy gave them the ground. She had so much property by then, she just gave it to them.

Well one time I asked Mama, I said, "Mama, don't you feel funny sitting there with all those educated ladies?" And Kate said, "No, I don't feel funny." So I said, "What do you do when they're talking about all those things you don't know nothing about?" And Kate said, "I keep my mouth shut and listen, that's what I do; as long as I keep my mouth shut they can think all they want to that I'm a fool. If I open my mouth and try to talk about something I don't know nothing about, I would prove it."

Kate's statement about the "educated ladies" was usually told in concert with another story. This was the story of "How Albert Learned To Sign His Name." We were taught to value a formal education and not to take it for granted. This is one of the few stories that provided us with insights into the strength and determination of our grandfather Albert.

How Albert Learned To Sign His Name

Mama used to tell us how Papa learned to sign his name. See, Albert always took his money to the bank and he had to sign what they call banknotes. But Albert couldn't write, so he always had to put his X where the signature was supposed to go. So one day Albert told Caddy and Kate that one thing he was going to learn to do before his children were old enough to go to school was to learn to write his name and go to the bank and sign his name to those banknotes. So Papa got what they call the old blue-back spelling book, I got it upstairs.

Well, anyway, Papa spent hours after work sitting at the kitchen table trying to figure out how to spell his name. Caddy and Kate used to sit there with him and watch him and see if he could do it. They would always tell him, "Go ahead, Albert, you can do it, go ahead, Albert, you can do it!" Well, finally one night Albert looked up and said he believed he got it. They were real happy. So anyway, the next time Albert went to the bank all three of them went together. Caddy and Kate went with

Albert
(1912)

him so they could watch him sign his name! *So when it came time to sign the X to the banknote, Caddy and Kate stood there and watched while Albert signed his name. Mama said she and Caddy were so proud standing there watching Papa sign his name. Mama said she never saw Caddy so proud and happy. Caddy was as proud as she could be. She was proud of Albert and when it was over she looked at Albert and she said, "Well, Albert, that's one X you will never have to sign no more."*[5]

Statements like Kate's remark about the value of silence have long been a favorite method of teaching in our family. In some instances the old sayings are part of a story; in other instances they are used independently. If there is no family story that adequately illustrates the message in the saying, a true-life experience of someone outside of the family is used. It is important that the story be true, for these aphorisms are taken seriously.

One of my favorite sayings is attributed to Caddy. It is "Never lift a man so high as to allow him to piss in your face." This taught us to value ourselves and not to let other people use us.

The following story illustrates the manner in which this was done. It teaches that while exposure to books is valuable, it does not mean that one is necessarily "educated." An educated person not only has the same sort of manners for everyone; he is endowed with the most venerated kind of intelligence: plain old common sense.

The Educated Fool

You know there was this girl in Lynchburg who I grew up with. Well it was just she and her mother. So I know for a fact that her mother took in washing and scrubbed floors and worked like a dog to get that girl through normal school so she could be a teacher. Well the girl finished and she became a teacher but she still lived with her mother. So she used to have her educated friends come over to her house for socials and things. Well, her mother used to love to sit in the parlor and talk along with them. But she couldn't speak good English and she used to talk like ordinary people talk. Do you know that that girl told her mother that she wasn't educated enough to sit and talk with her educated friends? She told her mother that she embarrassed her splitting up verbs and things!" She told her mother that when her educated friends came to visit her that she had to go in the kitchen. *And she was ashamed of her own mother. And do you know, her mother was so sad, but she went in the kitchen anyway. Every time her daughter had her friends over, her mother would just get up and go in the kitchen. Everybody in Lynchburg was talking about that thing. I know if I had been her mother, I wouldn't have gone in the kitchen. I would have asked her if her educated friends had scrubbed floors and washed clothes so she could speak* good *English. No, I don't like that.*

I don't like that. I don't do things for people because I expect anything from them and I don't believe in reminding children what you have done for them. But she wouldn't have sent me to the kitchen. [6]

"The Grapefruit and the Orange" demonstrates the value of common sense and intelligence. It is still one of Maggie's favorite legends. It not only shows that selfishness sometimes interferes with common sense; it was used along with innumerable other stories to remind us that there was no such thing as the "good old days" for black people. While we had common sense enough to know that we did not have money for everything, at least we had more money than Maggie did when she was a child. She told us this story over and over again. Maggie enjoyed telling this story. It was not one of my favorites because at the time it seemed to me that Maggie was trying to convince me that I should be grateful for sweetened grapefruits when what I wanted was money.

When I told the story to Susan her only reaction was surprise that there was ever a time when her grandmother did not know the difference between a grapefruit and an orange.

The Grapefruit and the Orange—Version I

I remember the first time I ever saw a grapefruit. It was one day when William and I were on our way to school. William saw it first; it was on a fruit stand on the white side of town. William said, "Look, Maggie, look at that big old orange." I looked, and I said, "William, I never saw such a big orange before." William said "Me neither, I sure would like to have me one of those big oranges." I said, "Me too," and we walked on to school still thinking about that big old orange. I thought about it all day and so did William. When we left school that day, I said, "William, let's ask the man how much one of those big oranges cost." William said, "I bet they cost a plenty money." So we stopped just long enough to ask the man how much it cost. I forget how much it was, but it was a lot of money for those days. Anyway, I said, "William, let's save our pennies and buy one." And William said, "We would have to save forever if we would ever get one," but William said he was going to ask Papa when he had his little nip and maybe Papa would give us some money. Well, we saved and saved those pennies but we knew we would never get enough money to buy one.

Now Prince was taken out of school and put to work because he was the oldest boy and we needed the money. Because he couldn't go to school he was allowed to keep some of his pay. So we knew he had money, but he was as stingy as he could be, so we didn't want to ask him. He probably would want almost all of it anyhow. But we didn't have any choice. So one day we told Prince about the big orange we had seen and told him that we were trying to save our pennies to buy one. We told him that if he wanted in that he could have half if he paid for it and we would take the other half. He said "uh huh" or something like that but he didn't say nothing else, so we just forgot all about him. Well, finally we had enough money and it was a Saturday and we asked Kate if we could take a walk. We planned to buy one of those oranges and go to the woods and eat it so we *wouldn't have to give anybody none. Well, we were on our way, and who should we meet but Prince. Prince said, "Where you all going?" and we told him we were going to buy us one of those big oranges and we weren't going to give him one bite because he was so stingy. And he looked kinda funny and he said, "No you ain't." We said, "It's our money." And that's when he told us what he had done and why he didn't want to let us spend our money for nothing. He said those things were as sour as they could be. We said, "How do you know, you never had one." And then he told us that when we told him about those big old oranges he went to see for himself. And sure enough, he bought one. And since he didn't want to give anybody none either, he went in the woods all by himself and peeled it and started to eat it. He said that thing was so sour it turned his lips inside out, but he ate it anyhow because it cost him his money. He said it wasn't no orange, it was called a grapefruit. He told us to go ahead and buy one if we didn't believe him. But we believed him, he was no liar. And he did not believe in wasting good money and he did not want us to waste our good money on a sour grapefruit. I was some disappointed.*

The next version of "The Grapefruit and the Orange" was collected from my great-niece Tondhi in 1974 when she was five years old. Today, at age eight, she does not remember this version. Since I did not have a tape recorder with me when Tondhi first told me this story, I wrote it down immediately after I heard it. I knew then that it would never be told the same way again. Recently Tondhi was asked why she liked this story; she replied: "Because it is a good story."

The Grapefruit and the Orange—Version II

Once there was a time when my grand. . . m-o-ther had never seen a, wait. [Long, thoughtful pause.] Well you know, she was my real grandmother and she had never seen a grapefruit in her whole life. And she was walking to school holding hands with this man called William and she said, "Look, William, look at

Prince
(1912)

that big grapefruit over there." And William looked and he said, "Boy, Mom, I have never ever seen a grapefruit as big as that. You?" And she said, "Me neither." So my grandmother and the man decided, you know, to save up their pennies to buy the grapefruit. And it was sour, them days. So they went in the woods and they met a prince, and the prince told them not to buy the grapefruit. Now how did he know it would turn their lips inside out? Well he knew because he was a sneaky prince. He had bought him a grapefruit and was not going to give my grand . . . m-o-ther one bite. Not one bite. And my grand . . . m . . . er-Mom was so-o-o mad, so she said she was going to buy something else with her pennies and she and the man William left too. Were his lips turned inside out for real, Aunt Kathryn?

While "The Grapefruit and the Orange" is a true story, innumerable stories that masqueraded as family stories were thinly disguised lies. These lies provide us with entertainment. I call them "anonymous cousin" stories. The "anonymous cousin" is a clue that the story itself is either an outright lie, or is grossly exaggerated. If I remember correctly, I first heard the following version of "Philadelphia: The 'Titty' of Brotherly Love" as a young adult. It was told by my Uncle Jimmie. In 1976 I asked Uncle Jimmie if he remembered telling the story to me. He replied that he did remember and added, "Girl, I could tell you a lot of things about the 'Titty' of Brotherly Love in those days."

Philadelphia: The "Titty" of Brotherly Love

It was our cousin, see, yes, oh I don't know when it happened, but he saw this happen with his own eyes. You know, long time ago, Philadelphia had two street car conductors, yes. One drove the trolley and the other one stood in a little square box-like thing, oh it only came up to his waist, and he used to collect the fares. See, that was before they had any colored folks on the bus lines driving, they had to have a riot in Philadelphia before they would let colored folks drive the buses. Well you know in those days you didn't pay when you got on, you got on the front and got off the back; this little booth was in the middle. Now if you wanted to sit in the back that was all right, you could just pay and sit in the back, but the street car wasn't like it is now, you couldn't get off the back you know, the side entrance, unless you had paid. The middle conductor pulled the cable that opened the door and you could only get off through the middle door.

Well, anyway, one day he [the cousin] said he was sitting on the street car and this big fat black woman got on with a little baby and she paid and sat in the back, right next to the conductor. Well, the baby started to cry, you know. So the woman tried to keep the baby quiet, and everybody was looking at her, he said. Well finally the woman pulled out her titty and tried to give it to the baby. Well, the baby wouldn't take it, but the conductor, the middle one, the minute she pulled out that big black juicy titty, looked like he couldn't keep his eyes off that titty, he just stared at it like a hungry rat stares at a piece of cheese. So the woman said to the baby, "Come on, honey, take this titty." But the baby didn't want it, and it kept on crying. And so the woman tried again, you know, she said, "Come on, honey, you better take this titty now." But the baby wouldn't take the titty. Well, the conductor could hardly collect the fares, he was so busy looking at this black titty. So the woman saw him looking so she looked down at the baby and she said, "Now come on, honey, come on and take your titty because if you don't I'm goin' to have to give it to the conductor." Everybody on the street car started laughing and the conductor turned red, white, blue and purple. He pulled the cord right in the middle of the block and put the woman off the street car, right up in the north! Right in the City of Brotherly Love, put her out right in the middle of the block!

When our cousin came home and told us about this story, that's when we started calling it "Philadelphia: The 'Titty' of

Brotherly Love." . . . *No, I don't know, I don't remember when we first started calling Philadelphia the "titty" of brotherly love. I know any time they stop a trolley car in the middle of the block like that and put that colored woman off you're crazy if you think you're going to find any brotherly love, yeah [laugh], didn't even give the poor woman time to put her titty back, put her off with her titty hanging out, right in the street.*

In at least two other versions of the story, collected from other members of the family, the story follows the same theme. Only the details change, depending a great deal upon the reactions of the listeners. For example, other versions say, "The poor woman didn't have a penny in her pocket," or "It was raining cats and dogs," or "It was one hundred and ten degrees in the shade." The woman is described as so poor she had holes in the *top* of her shoes, or as ragged or dressed in rags. Or "She was five, ten, or fifteen miles from home." "Her titty hung down to her knees!" "The baby was white!"[7]

"Philadelphia: The 'Titty' of Brotherly Love" demonstrates the way family legends may convey messages in comic garb. They are told primarily for entertainment; this one demonstrates that in some instances they are far from politically or socially neutral. The idea that "honest" racism existed in the South and "hidden" racism existed in the North was beaten and battered to death in a number of the fictionalized stories told to us even as children.

A number of these stories were based on true-life experiences which were masked with the "anonymous cousin," to keep us from knowing who was actually involved. The next legend was told to us as children. Despite its comic garb, it had its own subtle message.

Sleeping on the couch in the dining room meant that you had to sleep surrounded by Kate's nine black cats. In addition, you had to get up at 4:00 A.M. and help Kate feed them. We were led to believe that Kate had all kinds of ways to make children behave, even though they were teenagers. The next legend makes this explicit. "Miss Kate's couch" refers to Kate's routine. She took a nap from two o'clock until exactly three o'clock each day on the couch. Kate was called "Miss Kate" by all her friends and acquaintances, and by the other children in the neighborhood.

Why Our Cousin from the Country Had To Sleep on Miss Kate's Couch

He didn't mind nobody. He would stay out late at night and roam all over town and come home when he pleased. Kate knew he was afraid of ghosts and spirits and she decided to try to scare him into coming home before dark. So we had this swing on the front porch and one night Kate wrapped herself up in a sheet and sat in the porch swing making sounds like a sick ghost; she was groaning. So when Jack [fictional name] came up on the porch he looked over at the swing and said, "Hello, Cousin Kate, what's the matter, don't you feel good?" Well Kate didn't answer but she was mad enough. So the next night when he came home Kate was sitting in the swing all wrapped up in the sheet again but she wasn't saying nothing. So Jack walked up on the porch as bold as you please and said, "Good evening, Cousin Kate, isn't it a lovely evening?" He was just a laughing, they say. So Kate didn't say a word and Jack went on upstairs to his room in the attic, like. He was the oldest and he had a room to himself up there. They say he was just a laughing to himself and he got undressed and he was a humming and mumbling to himself; he was very pleased with himself; he was about seventeen then, I guess.

Well, he sat down on the bed and they say he got off his clothes and sat on the bed, happy like, and he was sitting there on the side of the bed in his bare feet when a big black snake hand reached out from under the bed and closed over one of his feet; it nearly scared him to death. He hollered so loud he woke up the whole house. They say he fell down the steps and ran out on the porch naked as a jaybird, and there was Kate sitting on the porch swinging in that white sheet, not saying a word. And he was a babbling and carrying on just like he wasn't a grown up man of seventeen.

Kate just got up and left him standing on the porch stark naked like that. He was scared to stay outside and scared to go inside and he wasn't about to go back up in his room. So he went to Albert and Kate's bedroom, and Albert came to the door and saw him standing there naked and bawled him out for not having the decency to cover himself in front of Miss Kate and the rest of the children. We had all been wakened up by all that noise, and none of us could believe our eyes, when we saw Jack standing up there naked shaking like it was cold outside. Then when he saw all of us, especially the girls, looking at "you-know-what," he didn't know what to do. So he tried to hide himself. And William said it looks like our cousin had to pee so bad that he was jumping around from one foot to another. So Kate came out and told him to go upstairs to bed. But he wouldn't go. So she told him he could sleep in the dining room on her couch but if he was going to come in the house late at night like that and wake up the whole house with all his noise and his imagination gone wild, he didn't deserve a room of his own. He was ready to promise anything. So Kate told him from now on he had to sleep in the dining room on the couch; she would put some of the other children in his room. None of us wanted it either. But she sent us back to bed and the very next day she made him start sleeping on the couch in the dining room. We were scared too, but Kate told us that the reason our cousin was acting like he had seen a ghost was because he knew he was wrong! and his imagination had played tricks on him.

Now, we tried to figure out what happened to our cousin that night, but once he got himself together he didn't want to talk about it any more, and Kate told us not to talk about it any more. But it went all over the neighborhood anyway, and Jack was just as nice and polite to Kate as he could be. She didn't *have a minute's trouble out of the rest of us, either, because we believed that she could make those hands come out from under our beds any time she wanted to. We never did get that thing straightened out, but I believe it was Caddy under that bed. I believe that Kate and Caddy planned the whole thing, and since Caddy was so little it was easy for her to crawl under that bed and wait for Jack to come in and grab onto his foot like that. And it was just as easy for her to slip out of the house during all the commotion, but I'm just guessing about Kate and Caddy.*

Even when I was grown and asked Mama about that night she still said Jack got what he deserved. Poor Jack never knew whether it was his imagination or not, but he swore that he thought he felt that hand grab on to his foot. The thing that makes me think it was somebody who was in there was the fact that somebody knew that Jack was humming and singing and laughing that night and somebody spread the story all over the neighborhood and made Jack look like a fool. It sounds just like something Caddy would do. But I wouldn't put it past Mama, either. [8]

Maggie never underestimated the power of unseen forces in the universe or Caddy and Kate's ability to make unusual, magical things happen. However, her unwavering conviction in the power of prayer and the existence of God was not to be confused with scary tactics. The next three legends provide concrete evidence of the strength of Maggie's beliefs. I was too young to remember the first incident, but I was an adult when Maggie told me of the other two occurrences. The last two experiences happened when Maggie was sent to Kate for consolation after my brother, R. C., died. The first one took place in Lynchburg; the second one happened in Philadelphia almost immediately after Maggie's visit with Kate.

All three of these stories have become a part of the family legends both for adults and for children.

The Nice Lady

When you were a little girl, no, you were a good-sized girl, you were very sick. The doctor said you might die. He left and said that he would be back the next day. Well, you slept through the night and you know me, I was so worried. Well, the next morning I was in the kitchen getting a cup of coffee and I looked around and there you were, standing in the kitchen saying you were hungry. I couldn't believe it. You were just as well as you could be; no fever, nothing. You asked me, "Mama, who was that nice lady who sat by me all night and put her hands on me and told me that I would be all right, that she was going to make me better?" I said, "What lady?" You described Caddy, down to her shawl! You had never seen Caddy or a picture of her, or anything, but you saw Caddy that night. [9]

A Heaven Full of Hoodlums

I was sitting there thinking of R. C. and crying, you know, in the kitchen with Kate. I just couldn't seem to get myself together. I kept asking: Why? Mama, why? If there is a God in heaven why did He take my child while those hoodlums and old people are still living? Why didn't He take me instead? God knows no mother should suffer like this. Losing a child. Nineteen and sick all the time, then he gets well . . .

I remember Kate was standing over the stove, and I could hardly hear her. But I remember what she said. She looked right at me and she said, "What you think, Maggie? You think God wants only hoodlums and old folks up there in heaven with Him? Maggie, don't you think that the good Lord wants some young folks and some good folks up in heaven with him as well as a heaven full of hoodlums and old people? He takes the good, the bad, and the old and the young. Maggie, He didn't take you because it ain't your time yet. When your time comes, He'll take you. He's trying to tell you something, Maggie. You got *other children and a husband. Who's going to take care of them, me? No. My time may be any time; I'm too old.*

Well, I came on back to Philadelphia and tried to make it.

The Message

This is the God's truth. I was laying up in the bed, crying. I was thinking about Donald and Reggie being overseas and that they may be killed and buried over there. I just couldn't think of my sons all caught up in wars, for what? So I heard the bell ring and I said, Oh my Lord, you know, it was too late for anybody to come by.

Well, Marie [a friend] answered the door and she said she saw this strange-looking woman on the porch, and that she was crying. So she thought something was wrong with her, you know. But she told her that she had a message for a Mrs. Marjorie Lawson, and it was an important message of good news, and she was told to tell it to nobody but me. Well, Marie said she started to tell her that she would see, you know. But the woman said she knew where I was, and before Marie knew what happened she was on her way upstairs.

So I looked up and there was this strange white woman I had never seen in my life by my bed, crying. Before I could open my mouth she said, "I have a message from your son, R.C. He said to tell you that he was very happy where he was, and for you not to worry about him, but that he was coming back to you. This time he wouldn't be sick, and he would be a girl." And she described R. C. to a T. Next thing I knew, that woman was gone. I never saw her again in my life, but you know, I believed her. I got up out of that bed that night. And when Donald's child was born I could hardly wait. It was a girl. I held it in my arms and looked into that baby's eyes. Those were R. C.'s eyes staring up at me. The good Lord had answered my prayers and sent my child back to me. [10]

In these legends the past is not kept alive merely for its own sake but rather for the purpose of informing the present. Ancestors, parents and others appear with human frailties as well as human strengths. They are realistic human beings rather than symbolic abstractions. Even God is a divine and all-knowing deity who is touchable and responsive to the sincere prayer of mortals who do not spend their lives merely hating (yet imitating) what they despise.

III
Maggie's Stories
of "Color" and "Race"

Maggie and husband Raphael Lawson
(1919)

Introduction

One night quite recently I was visiting Maggie and we were watching the late show on television. Lana Turner was starring in a movie version of Fannie Hurst's novel, *Imitation of Life*, one of those books about the plight of the "poor mulatto," a stereotype still thrust upon white-skinned blacks.[1]

In the movie Peola was a good-sized girl when she discovered that she was different. By different, I mean she was different from most blacks, those of us who are visible. Like many white-skinned blacks, Peola was a "marginal"—she was rejected by the white world of race, and she was rejected by the black world of race, because Peola let it be known that she did not want to be part of an "inferior" race. Peola had a black *mother*. This is typical. Usually, it is supposed that it is the mother not the father who is black. But Peola's mother was not a "loose black hussy" type. No. She was dark, and, to me, beautiful. She was pleasingly plump, old-fashioned, rather dowdy, and devoted to her daughter.

One day Peola went to a new school. None of her classmates knew she had her one blot of black blood. In other words, Peola was "passing." It started to rain. Not just rain, but Hollywood rain, a Hollywood downpour. Naturally, little Peola's mother did not want Peola to get wet. So she dragged herself out Hollywood style, weary, worn, wet, and worried.

Now Peola's mother stood outside the window inside the school, and peeked in at Peola. Peola's mother was all dressed in black, including her hat. She was a big, dripping-wet black woman with sad eyes, smiling and trying to get Peola's attention. She wanted Peola to know she had brought her an umbrella. The mother was a messed-up mosaic of greyish blackness. She was smiling sadly, with clown-eyed sadness. Finally, she was noticed by Peola's teacher, and Peola looked, and saw *it*. The big black finger pointing at her. The finger, sociologists infer, cries out, "nigger," bringing with it the terror of discovery for those who "cross over" deliberately. And the black finger pointing at Peola was her mother's finger.

Now, Peola was not smart. She could have pulled off her "passing" act. All she had to do was turn to her classmates and explain, "Oh, look, 'Aunt' Jane brought me my umbrella, she's just like one of the family, you know." Those children would have understood. That's all Peola had to do. But no. Peola, panic-stricken, jumped from her seat, shamed, head hung low. She passed her mother and quickly walked out. Her mother stood, rain-soaked and dripping with tears, until with two umbrellas, she stumbled off in the rain. "Passing" Hollywood style is so sad, I thought to myself.

Then Maggie spoke. She was not angry. She was calm. She said, "If that little gal had been part of our family, she would have had her ass beat to a fare-thee-well and been given a one-way ticket to Canada on the first thing moving out." In other words, if she wouldn't be black, she would have been made to "cross over," like some of our younger cousins second removed who suddenly disappeared. Then Maggie got up and went to bed.

There are no stories of "cross-overs" in the book. Why? Because there are no "cross-overs" among the Gordons. A family member who "crosses over" is considered dead. Gone. Unmourned. Under no circumstances are they to contact the family. No white-skinned member of the Gordon family ever "crossed over." "Keeping the color" has been a long-standing practice in our family.

Stories

In the families of the Gordons, and their cousins, the Carsons, white-skinned, blue-eyed, black children like my mother Maggie were as common as corn pone and collard greens. Everybody knew that the wrath of God, Caddy, and Kate fell upon any white-skinned member of the Gordon family who *dared* to use the term "black" in a derogatory fashion.

White skin could be a help or a handicap, depending upon the circumstances. In the first story here, it was a handicap. My brothers and I were told this story as we were growing up. I thoroughly enjoyed it for all the wrong reasons. I wished Maggie had looked like the big black "mammies" in the movies. I thought at the time that she would have treated me the way Shirley Temple's black "mammies" treated Shirley. I confided this secret wish to Maggie, who immediately stopped me from going to what she called the "nigger eyestraining section" of the segregated movies to have my mind warped by all that "nonsense." I, for one, was as happy as I could be whenever she told this story. I was glad she had been punished for being "white."

This incident was one of many similar stories remembered by Maggie from the time when she was a child of six or seven, living in Lynchburg. She told it for the first time to my daughter Susan in 1966, when Susan was ten years old. I have called the story "God and Lice."

God and Lice

I had a lot of trouble when I was a child that was because I was light. Yes, because I looked like white I wasn't liked. I used to hate the black children sometimes because they were mean to me. They would call me names and say I wasn't for real. "At least I'm real," they would say, and I would say back, "You're a black nigger, that's what you are," and I would call them "Blackies! Blackies! Nappy-headed blackies!" You know, I was only a child; I couldn't help it. And they knew I would get a whipping, and they would run to Mama and say, "Miss Kate, Miss Kate, Maggie called me black again!" Mama wouldn't even listen to my side; I got a whipping practically every day for calling somebody black; and they never got a whipping for calling me "unreal" or calling me "you white thing you" or anything. Even "poor white trash"!—and that was the worst thing they could think of, you know!

So I used to try to make friends with them, so I would say, "Come over to my house and let me comb your hair." See, we didn't have anybody in our house that didn't have "good" hair, you know, and I used to love to comb and plait their hair so they would treat me nice. Mine was so fine that it wouldn't stay plaited and you know all my cousins and my sisters had that fine hair that wouldn't stay plaited. But I would do all kinds of things for those children so they wouldn't tell on me when I called them black.

Kate couldn't stand a liar and looked like she could smell a lie. So I had to tell the truth. She'd say, "Maggie, did you call them children black again?" And I would say, "Yes, Ma'am," and that's as far as she would let me get. She tried to whip me so hard that I would stop calling the other children black, but I would call them black anyway, because I couldn't help it. I would be so mad! I wasn't but about seven years old, a little thing, and I sure couldn't help looking like I did.

Caddy was a whipper too, and she would've killed me if she

had known about it. Her mother Liza was as black as coal; she had straight hair down to her waist; I remember her [Caddy] and I sure remember those whippings I used to get for calling those children black. And I could handle that nappy hair, too, I could cornroll and everything. I forgot how to do it now, but we didn't have any straightening combs in those days like we do now. So those children's mothers used to like it when I combed their hair. And I used to want them to be my friends and I used to try to think up nice things to do for them.

One day I said to one of them, "Would you like to comb my hair?" And she said, "No! My mama told me not to get near your hair." And I said, "Why?" And she said, "You got lice in your hair, that's why." I said I didn't, and she said I had white folks' hair and that lice lived in white folks' hair and they couldn't live in real black *folks' hair because they would smother to death! And I said they sure would in all those old nappy naps, that God Almighty Himself would smother to death if He had to live on the head of a "black nappy-headed nigger," much less lice.*

Well, I never will forget that whipping, it was two whippings and a promise. I got them all. One from Kate, not only for calling the girl black and nappy-headed but for comparing God with a louse. Not only that, I said God would smother to death like a louse if He had to live on the head of a "black nappy-headed nigger." And Kate said, "Did you say that, Maggie?" And I said, "Yes, Ma'am." There wasn't any way I could've straightened that thing out. [2]

One thing stood out in my memory when my mother told this story. When she told it she seemed to forget for a moment that I had "bad" hair, and *somebody* had warned me as a child going to school *not* to sit too near to white children in school because they had lice in their hair and the lice might jump over to mine. And I was also told not to worry about it too much because it was *highly unlikely* that they would live very long in nappy hair like mine because they would *smother to death*. And I remember being warned that it just wasn't worth the chance of sitting next to white children and getting infected with lice, it was as simple as that. When Maggie was going to school, there was no question of sitting next to white children—she was the whitest thing in the room, with the straightest hair. According to Maggie, the black children used to avoid her hair like the plague. I remember thinking to myself as a child, I guess they didn't want to catch lice then, either.

I am reminded of the words of Jean Finot. "The conception of races once so innocent," he says, "has cast a veil of tragedy over the earth. From without it shows us humanity divided into unequal fractions. . . . From within this same falsely conceived science of races likewise encourages hatred and discord among the children of the same common country. . . . People against people, race against race . . . persecution and extermination on every hand."[3] And, I may add, not only among children of the same country but among black children and black adults of the same exploited caste. Maggie's story of "God and Lice" shows how we take the nomenclature of oppression and apply it to ourselves.

The next story is Maggie's first experience with "passing." In 1916, next to census takers, train attendants and train conductors must have been thought to be among the finest physical anthropologists in the nation. It also must have been assumed that they were kissing cousins to God; they were expected to *look at* and *look through* a person, to determine whether or not the individual had his or her "qualifying" or "disqualifying" drops of "blood," and to decide in which coach they should sit.

In all fairness to the train conductors, however, it must be noted that at the time Maggie was a sweet sixteen-year-old girl with white skin and a body that even the fashions of 1916 could not completely obscure. She had also been trained during summer visits to Philadelphia in the fine art of "passing" when expedient by the family experts, our cousins, the Carsons.

Maggie
(1916)

During this time, Cousin Dave had evidently returned to Lynchburg from Philadelphia and had come to the depot to put Maggie on the train. It must be remembered that it was impossible for either one of them to "pass" in *Lynchburg* and they never knew when they were being watched. "Passing" was a very dangerous business with the Carsons; they perceived themselves as truth-tellers and warriors, and they were closer than kissing cousins to the Gordons.

Jim Crow

I remember the first time I rode the train by myself coming to Philadelphia. Cousin Dave took me to the station, you know, he looked just like a white man, but he said, "Maggie, you never can tell, you look white but you better play it safe and sit in the Jim Crow car." So he got me a seat in the Jim Crow car, and it was filled, you know. Everybody had a shoebox full of food; we weren't allowed to eat in the dining cars. So Kate had fixed me my shoebox full of fried chicken and pound cake and everything, but the train car was stinking and as hot as it could be. But I didn't even think of moving.

Well, the colored people probably knew I was colored so they didn't even think anything about me being there. Soon the train pulled off and the conductor came around to pick up the tickets. Well, when he saw me sitting in the Jim Crow car he liked to had a fit. He came over to me and he said, "Miss, you are in the wrong car, this car is for niggers." I said, "It is?" He said, "Yes, you will have to move back in the white section."

Well, you know they put the Jim Crow car right up on the engine. And the colored folks pretended they didn't know what was going on. So the conductor was nice as he could be; he carried my bags to the white section and got me a nice seat. I carried my own shoebox, but I didn't see anybody else with a shoebox; anyway, they might have had shoeboxes but I wasn't taking any chances, so I waited until we had to change trains and I went in the white toilet and sat on a stool and ate a piece of my fried chicken. It was the first time I had "passed" by myself, but I didn't do it on purpose. I was pretty young, I guess no more than sixteen, and those white conductors were so nice to me, they really took good care of me, putting me on the right train to Philadelphia, carrying my bags and things, asking me if I was all right, and making sure I was comfortable. And the white people were so nice to me I couldn't help but laugh inside. It just goes to show you—I was just as colored as anybody else, only I didn't look colored.

So that's when I decided I would be white whenever I wanted to be, and colored whenever I wanted to be. They used to say that colored folks could tell other colored folks no matter what they looked like. I don't know if this is true or not; I know none of the colored folks ever gave me away if they did know.

How the Porter Almost Gave Up the Game

Well, I was sitting in the white car; did I tell you what happened? Well, we had gotten well out of Lynchburg when this man, this colored man from Lynchburg, you know, I knew him well . . . he was the porter who went through the white cars selling things, you know. Well, when he got to me, now I'm sitting there with all these white folks. He said, "Maggie! Maggie, what you doing here?" Well, I was too scared to open my mouth because all the white folks sitting around me started looking. So he caught on right away; he said, "Oh, I beg your pardon, Miss, I am sorry, I thought you was the daughter of the white lady I used to work for. I'm so sorry!" Well, I didn't say a word and the white folks went on back to whatever they were doing. But every time he came through the car he was grinning and waiting on those folks and saying, "Yes, Ma'am," and stuff. And he said, "Anything I can get you, Ma'am?" I didn't have any money so I said, "No, thank you." And he said, "Yes, Miss," and went on just like we didn't know each other well. He was one of Prince's good friends and was in our house all the time.

Well, when I got off in Washington, D.C., he was standing in the station just grinning, watching those white conductors carrying my bags and stuff. Later on when I went home to visit we used to sit in the kitchen and laugh at that one. He said, "Maggie, I sure almost gave up the game that time!" I told him I didn't do it, the conductors did. He said, "Well, Maggie, I know one thing, I'll never make a mistake like that again, but I was some surprised to see you sitting in that white car!"[4]

Another narrow escape with a train conductor was the famous incident involving Walter White, when he was the Executive Director of the NAACP. It was discovered in one of the small Southern towns where he was investigating a lynching that he was a white-skinned black. He was on his way to a meeting of whites who had participated in this practice. He was stopped on the street by a black man who told him to rush and catch the train that was just about to leave town. White had been discovered to be black. White recalls that he made the train with one minute to spare. As he boarded the train he was asked by a white trainman why he was leaving town before the fun began. White asked, "What fun?" The train conductor replied that the townspeople planned to "take care" of a "nigger" who was "passing for a white man, who had been collecting information concerning lynching."[5] "Passing" can be a harrowing experience when it is done for economic, political, or social justice (espionage) purposes. When it is done for non-essential reasons it can be comical or absurd, as in the next example.

In New York before the Depression, at the time the nightclub circuit discovered the talents of the black entertainer, some blacks would attempt to pass for white in order to get into the nightclubs. The nightclub owners assumed that one black person could "spot" another, regardless of how "white" he looked, so they hired black "spotters." These "spotters" would point out blacks who were "passing" and throw them out. They would be bounced.[6]

With the onset of the Depression, most blacks could not afford to eat, much less run to downtown New York to nightclubs. So the black "spotters" had no one to "spot." To keep from losing their jobs, they would pay white-skinned blacks to come downtown, try to "pass," and be "spotted" and bounced.

But things really got tight, and the "spotters," those "spotted" and the nightclub owners too, all blew up together in one equal opportunity economic explosion, the holocaust called the stock market crash. And that was the end of the fine art of "spotting."

Maggie's legends of "color" and "race" skip from 1916 to 1938. In 1938 Philadelphia was still segregated in its public accommodations such as restaurants, theatres, and neighborhood movies. Whole neighborhoods had changed with dramatic speed from white to black as whites fled to the suburbs, abandoning homes, schools and churches to the growing influx of educated, race-conscious black migrants from the South. De facto segregation became the way of life. It was most evident in residential patterns in which small groups of "middle-class" blacks were surrounded by large groups of middle and lower-class whites.

By this time Maggie had married, and had borne her four children. The neighborhood to which we moved was an almost totally black enclave. There were only three white residents left. One was an old Italian woman who was seldom seen. Legend had it that she had lost all her money in the stock market crash of 1929 and was too poor to move. When the first blacks moved into the block she went indoors and remained there. The two other whites were an elderly "Anglo-Saxon" couple named Winters. Again, according to legend, it was reported that the block busters came to Mr. Winters' home and urged him to put his house up for sale at once. They told him they expected the whole block would be overrun by "niggers" in the next two weeks, and he is said to have been outraged. Community legend reports he replied, "You get the hell off my front porch; I'm not selling my house just because my neighbors are changing colors! When I leave my house I will be carried out feet first." Maggie loved the story. She told us to respect Mr. Winters. We did. And despite the growing resentment of the blacks in our neighborhood toward all whites, Mr. Winters was respected by all. He was not doing us any favors, we knew that. He remained in splendid isolation from us. He never visited us, nor we him. He was never visited by other whites. I understand he lived in that house long after we moved again; in fact, his wife died and they carried her out feet first. Then he died and they carried him out feet first. Only then did his house go up for sale. I remember how he used to tip his hat to me in our brief encounters and say, "Good afternoon, little Miss Lawson." I would reply, "Good afternoon, Mr. Winters." At that time I was called by my peers Kathryn Liver-Lipped Lawson of Lepersville. Lepersville was my house.

What does all this have to do with our family folklore? First of all, Mr. Winters is remembered for his declaration of independence. It was a declaration more meaningful to us than Abraham Lincoln's Gettysburg Address. When we were told about Mr. Winters, we were also reminded that when Abraham Lincoln referred to "our fathers," he was not talking about *our* fathers; he was not speaking to *us*. Mr. Winters was. More important, we were ripe and ready to hate *all* white people; all blacks in our neighborhood were ready, except Maggie, and she kept Mr. Winters dangling in our vision. Maggie's attitude toward "race" and "color" in 1938 was why our house was called "Lepersville." Maggie had friends of all colors, creeds, occupations, and dispositions, and whether her black neighbors liked it or not, they were always welcome in our house.

Maggie's best friend was an Italian who was married to a West Indian. Her name was Marie, and she is the only white person I know personally who tried to pass for black. She plays an important role in Maggie's accounts of "color" and "race." Maggie made us call her "aunt" and Marie told everybody that she was Maggie's sister. She and Maggie used to pass for white together to spite the segregation laws. I venture to speculate that Maggie also thought she was spiting the people in our neighborhood for their attitudes towards Marie. They were passing for white the night in 1938 when Joe Louis knocked out the German, Max Schmeling.

Joe Louis

You know, Marie and I used to go downtown to the movies any time we wanted, and we would always sit smack in the middle of the white section, downstairs. That's when the colored had to sit up in the peanut gallery, yes, right up here in Philadelphia, they had a peanut gallery, up in the attic of the theatre, and all the colored folks had to sit up there. Well honey, I remember this night, they stopped the show right in the middle, and a man walked out on the stage and announced that Joe Louis had knocked out Max Schmeling. Marie and I jumped up and down and started hollering and screaming and clapping our hands and hugging each other. All of a sudden we looked around and all the white folks were looking at us like we were crazy. Wasn't nobody hollering and screaming but us and the other niggers in the peanut gallery! That was something, I tell you. We sat down fast but we were as happy as we could be. We couldn't wait to get home and celebrate with the rest of the folks. I don't think we even stayed long enough to see the rest of the picture, we were so happy. [7]

Mussolini came to power in Italy in 1922; by 1935 he had invaded Ethiopia; in 1936 Hitler had clearly stated his doctrine of "pure Aryan" races. That same year he refused to honor two black Olympic stars, Jesse Owens and Ralph Metcalf, in Berlin. Then, to top it off, that same year Max Schmeling knocked out Joe Louis, a man with whom blacks could identify. "Not until Louis gained complete revenge in 1938," writes John Hope Franklin, "could the average Negro speak of Nazis without a feeling of personal antagonism." [8]

Joel A. Rogers, historian and news analyst, was sent by the *Pittsburgh Courier* to cover the war. In his later writings he says:

> Even the most casual visitor to Italy cannot help but see that it is a land of very much mixed races. Nevertheless, on July 13, 1938, the Fascist Grand Council with one stroke of the pen, and without setting up a single face-bleaching or hair straightening parlor in Sicily, Calabria, or elsewhere, transformed the Italians into a "pure Aryan race."
> . . . In other words, Hannibal never crossed the Alps and the Latin writers who told of seeing him were liars. As for the Egyptians, the Moors, the Huns, and other dark-skinned non-Aryans, they only imagined they had entered Italy.[9]

Italy's invasion of Ethiopia was common knowledge among blacks in the United States.[10] It was the worst time for a lone Italian woman, an uneducated waitress with no sense of history or current events, to pass for black in a neighborhood like ours.

It may be argued that Marie was not trying to "pass," that she was only trying to be accepted by someone in our neighborhood.[11] The facts refute the argument. Marie was *planning* for her future as someone of importance in a black country in the West Indies. Her husband had assured her that if she would work and help him get through law school, as soon as he finished they would leave the country and return to his home. He had a high government post awaiting him; she could be his light-skinned "black" wife from the United States; this would be to his political advantage. With Maggie as her "sister" and us as "family," Marie could prove that she was black if it were necessary. Marie was not smart enough or conniving or cunning enough to think up such a plan; the plan was carefully concocted by her husband. Maggie's "color" helped and so did ours. And Maggie *knew it;* she never liked Marie's husband and she never trusted him. She told me this later; at the time she just insisted we call Marie "aunt." We did.

It soon came to pass that if Marie's husband was ever going to get to law school, then he would have to quit his job and go to school full time. Marie had to find a better job. One of the requirements for applying for a better job was a physical examination. And the physical examination included a specimen of urine. This one specimen of urine entered Maggie's accounts of "color" and "race." It happened in 1938, the story has remained alive; it has been passed from Maggie to me, from me to my daughter, and from Maggie to her grandson Donald.

I heard this story almost immediately after it happened; Maggie could not tell my father and she did not want to tell her friends. She had to tell *somebody*, for she was outraged; I remember her outrage to this day. "Miss Mary" was a black female pharmacist; to her Marie became public enemy number one the day she moved into the neighborhood, with a black husband who was educated and just about the right age for Miss Mary.

Urine and Pee

I know people don't like Marie just because she's white. But she is a good person. Miss Mary is spreading this story about Marie because she is white. You know what she's telling people? Well, you know when Marie went to get a new job she had to take a physical examination and the doctor asked her to bring in some urine. Now everybody in this block cannot make me believe they knew that urine was the same thing as pee before this happened. Not a soul in this block says, "I have to go urinate." They say, "I have to pee." So why is it so terrible because Marie didn't know that urine was pee?

Well anyway, Marie went to Miss Mary and said, "Miss Mary?" and Miss Mary said "Yaaas?" You know how snotty she can be. Well anyway, Marie said, "I would like ten cents worth of urine please." Miss Mary said "Whaaaat?" and Marie said, "I would like ten cents worth of urine please." Now, the drug store was full of people and Miss Mary did not have to do what she did in front of all those people. She said real loud, "You want TEN CENTS' WORTH OF URINE?" *and Marie, not knowing that everybody was listening, said, "Yes." Now Miss Mary could have been nice. She could have whispered in Marie's ear or something and told her what to do, but did she? No. Marie was white and she doesn't like her just for that. Marie never hurt anybody. Marie wouldn't hurt a soul. She has gone out of her way to be nice to these "niggers."*

Well anyhow, Miss Mary said real loud again, "WHAT DO YOU WANT TO BUY TEN CENTS' WORTH OF URINE FOR? MRS., AH, WHAT IS YOUR LAST NAME AGAIN?" *And she knew what Marie's last name was. So Marie told her that she had to have some urine to take in as part of a physical, and Miss Mary yelled,* "YOU WANT TO BUY TEN CENTS' WORTH OF URINE AS A SPECIMEN FOR A PHYSICAL EXAMINATION?" *and Marie said, "Yes, and if it costs more I'll pay for it."*

Well, that was the clicker, people started to laugh. Then Miss Mary said, "WELL, MRS. WHAT'S YOUR NAME, I'M SURE THEY DON'T WANT MINE!" *Well by that time the people were rolling on the floor just a laughing, but she didn't know why, so she just left. So she came here to me and she said, "Marge, why wouldn't the doctors want the urine if I bought it from Miss Mary's?" I said, "Marie, what are you talking about?" and then she told me what happened.*

Well, when I told Marie that urine was pee, she nearly died. She bawled like a baby. She was so ashamed of herself, I felt so sorry for her. And she said, "Oh, my God, Marge,[12] *suppose Louie hears about this, he will be so ashamed of me!" I said, "He's your husband and if he's ashamed of you just because you didn't know that urine is pee, he doesn't deserve a good wife like you, Marie." But you know Marie, she feels so inferior to educated people. And these educated "niggers" around here make me sick with that stuff. If some white woman had done to Miss Mary what Miss Mary did to Marie, Miss Mary would be hustling down to the NAACP with her coattails flapping in the wind, yelling prejudice at the top of her lungs!*

What stands out in my memory most vividly is how I hated the fact that we had to stop saying "piss" and "pee" and say "urinate." I had never heard the word "urinate" used in my house before. I had no idea that "urine" was the same thing as "piss" and "pee."

More important is the way Maggie stood by her friends while their enemies called them names. Marie was called "Marie, the dumb wop," behind her back, and this incident triggered a whole series of lies about what "Marie, the dumb wop," did. When Marie's husband finished law school he packed his things and left the country alone; he told Marie he would send for her as soon as he could. He never sent for her; he never wrote to her; he disappeared. Marie spent her days crying and playing pinochle with Maggie when she was not working. And she lingered with us a long time waiting and hoping for the summons that would make her "somebody." Finally Maggie convinced her that she had been "chewed up and spit out." She should go back to her own people and stop trying to be what she was not. Maggie told her "not to bear hate in her heart because hate would form a cancer on her soul."

And during World War II, Marie went back to the world of white folks, never to be heard from again.

And although I laughed when I re-examined this memory, it was a laughter tinged with guilt. Marie *was* a good person; she was very kind to us. And she did not have to be kind to us. We stopped calling her "aunt" and called her plain old "Marie" like she was our age. This was a signal of our disrespect for her and our hate for the Italians. We dared not call her a "dumb wop" even behind her back; we dared not use any derogatory ethnic terms; we were totally intimidated by Maggie's inherited ability to "smell" and to "taste" evil and by her "bops" in the mouth that left teeth aching for days. The preceding story reminds me of a place in Allport's *Nature of Prejudice* where he quotes a line from Byron: "If I laugh at any mortal thing, it is that I may not weep." [13]

The next story speaks directly to the time referred to in a dialogue in Jean Toomer's magnificent book, *Cane*, in which one character says to another: "There is no such thing as happiness. Life bends joy and pain, beauty and ugliness, in such a way that no one may isolate them. No one should want to. Perfect joy, or perfect pain, with no contrasting element to define them, would mean a monotony of consciousness, would mean death." [14]

As mentioned before, it was in World War II that Maggie lost her eldest son, my brother R. C. Her life was for a long time a constancy of perfect pain. When he died, she died in part; then the army took her second son, and finally her third son. I lived in another city and Maggie wrote me cheerful letters regularly, whether I answered or not. It was not until I returned to Philadelphia in the 1960s to live that I discovered that Maggie had changed. I think she remembers the next event, because it was a time when her patience with prejudiced white folks came to a screeching halt.

From the 1940s: On the Bus

You know one day, it was during the war, Donald was overseas and I was worried about him. I was riding the bus through our old neighborhood, you know. And the colored folks had taken over the whole neighborhood by then, so I was looking out of the window minding my own business and this white woman sat down next to me. So she saw me looking out the window; I was looking to see if I saw anybody I knew, you know. So she said to me, "Isn't it a shame, this used to be such a nice neighborhood before the 'niggers' took it over." Well, I was so mad all I could think about were R. C. lost, Donald and Reggie over in Europe—God knows where!—and I said, "What did you say?" And she said, "You know this used to be a real nice neighborhood before the 'niggers' took it over."

Well now, I don't usually cuss, so I said, "Listen, woman, I lost a black son and got two more over there fighting to save your big white ass. . . . " I thought she was going to die right there on the seat. She jumped up and ran to the front of the bus and I right behind her. Honey, she jumped off the bus right in the middle of that "nigger neighborhood" but she knew she was safer there than she was with me. I was just about to snatch her baldheaded, I was so mad!

The Friendly Customer

Well, you know when I went to work for Mr. H., well you know he knew I was colored but it didn't matter to him. I was the only colored in the shop. So I said to Mr. H., I said, "Mr. H., I think you better tell these people I'm colored." So he said, "Why should I tell them you're colored?" I said, "Because I don't want them to think I'm white, that's why." Mr. H. said, "I don't give a damn what you are, Marge, to me you are one of the best polishers I ever had. Anyway, it's none of their damn business what you are." So I said, "All right, it's up to you."

So there was a woman who always came in the shop. She was working in another jewelry store and she used to always bring a lot of business to us, you see. So she used to always come over and talk to me. She tried to be real friendly. So sometimes she used to drop by and one day she asked me to come go with her to lunch. Well, I told her I didn't go out to lunch, I ate my lunch in the shop. Well, she started to come over and visit and bring her lunch and eat with me and visit with me. Then she started to bring her lunch and we would eat lunch together practically every day. So we got to be friends.

So one day, I don't know how the subject came up, but this day I told her I was colored. Well, she looked so funny. She didn't say a word, but she could hardly eat her lunch she was so upset. So do you know she stopped bringing her business to Mr. H. and she never came in the shop from that day on. So I told Mr. H. that I told her I was colored and maybe that's why she didn't come in the shop any more. I didn't want to keep it from him. So he said he knew about it. I guess everybody knew about it in the shop by then, but it didn't make any difference to them. They treated me the same way they did before.

So I told Mr. H. that he lost a lot of business from that woman, and I didn't want to cause him to lose business. He said, "We don't need their business, Marge. We got more business than we can handle now." He said, "Marge, you are the best polisher I ever had and you do your work. I don't care about their business, and you shouldn't either. Never worry about anything that can be replaced."

Can you imagine! She never came back. But they sent their business back by somebody else. But I always remembered what Mr. H. said, not to worry about losing what can be replaced. One day I thought I had lost a valuable diamond and I was worried sick. That diamond was worth a lot of money. I was running around looking everywhere for that diamond. And Mr. H. said, "Marge, didn't I tell you not to worry about what can be replaced?" Well, that was some good advice. I don't worry about what can be replaced. He was Irish, I think. That woman was so friendly until she found out I was colored. Can you imagine? She never came near me again. I never saw her again and I worked for Mr. H. for years after that happened. [15]

Maggie Gordon Lawson is now a great-grandmother with fifteen grandchildren, all but one of whom were born and raised in Philadelphia. The one exception is my daughter Susan, who was born in Baton Rouge, Louisiana, and lived there until the age of three, when both of us returned to Philadelphia. Maggie still lives in Philadelphia surrounded by her extended family of children, grandchildren, wives, husbands, and her nieces, nephews, cousins, and their children, all of whom are equal in the eyes of God and Maggie. And in some way she has reached them all, maintaining a sort of homestead where each one has equal access to her traditions, her folklore, her philosophy of life, her strong and unwavering conviction in the omniscience of the good Lord, God Almighty, who is the prime mover of all mankind. She is affectionately called "Mom."

It was about nine years ago that Maggie started life anew. She moved into a modern apartment designed for people over sixty-five, and within a short time established a new network of friends of various colors, creeds, religions, and dispositions. She is the epitome of the blend of modernization and tradition. But in her own words, one thing she is not: that is what she calls an "old miss young." So she wears her pants-suits with considerable grace, smokes her cigarettes, cooks her good Southern food, reads her books, goes to the theatre, and to the Farmers Market twice a week. Once each year she goes "home." Home is Lynchburg, to visit her two surviving brothers, Jimmie and William, and their wives, children, and grandchildren—and a multitude of cousins, first, second, and third. She has become a family historian par excellance, but she is more than that. In her own way she is an activist; along with Martin Luther King and Malcolm X and thousands of others in the 1960s, Maggie became a special kind of warrior.

From the 1970s: Poor Stella Dallas

When I first moved into this apartment [housing for people over sixty-five] there wasn't many colored folks in here. I don't think there are many here now, but then there were hardly any. I was the first one, or one of the first ones, and I don't believe 'til this day that they knew I was colored. And my next door neighbor came and asked me. You know, she didn't care, but she was curious. She said, "Marge, are you colored?" and I said, "Yes, I am." And she said, "Well, God knows I couldn't tell." And I said, "Why did you ask me that?" And she said that somebody had told her that she had a colored neighbor and she said no colored had moved on the floor, in fact she had sworn to it. She thought it was funny.

Well, soon after I moved in several other colored people

Maggie
(1976)

moved in. There was no mistake about them, so by the time this happened about five or six coloreds were in the building. One day a new neighbor, a white widow, moved across the hall from me. Well, I used to speak to her like everybody else, you know, and she tried to be real friendly. She looked too much like Stella Dallas for me. [16] Well, she hadn't been here long and she came over to my apartment one morning and asked me to go shopping with her. Well, I was trying to make some excuse because I didn't want to be seen on the street with her, you know. But I didn't want to hurt her feelings so I told her I had something else to do but I invited her to have a cup of coffee. So she was sitting at the table here and she was talking and telling me how glad she was that she was living in the building. I wasn't paying much attention until she said, "You know, Marge, I have moved so many times, I had to move out of the house my husband left me, because 'niggers' took over the neighborhood; then I moved to Germantown and they took over the neighborhood again; I must have moved about five times trying to get away from them. I moved in here because I heard they had a quota on 'niggers' here, so I thought it would be safe here. Do you know how many 'niggers' are in the building, Marge?" So I looked at her and I made like I was thinking. I was thinking, all right. Then I said, "Well, now let me see, I guess there might be about five or six colored couples in the building, including me."

Well, I never will forget the look on her face, she was so nervous. She said, "Marge, are you a 'nigger?'" I said, "No, I am not a 'nigger,' I am a Negro and all my children are Jews!" I figured that if she hated "niggers" she hated Jews too, so that's why I said that.

Well, I almost felt sorry for her; she apologized and tried her best to swallow her words, but you know, Kate always said, you can't recall the spoken word, and she couldn't. Well, she left saying how much she wanted to be friends, and that she didn't mean any harm, you know, all that stuff. But I said, it was all *right, you know, I thought I was going to have to live across from her and I didn't relish hard feelings.*

Well, it wasn't too long before she moved. I guess when she found out that I was colored and all my children were Jews she just didn't know what to do. So she stayed locked up in her apartment for a while. Clara [a white neighbor] told me she ate a lot of oranges there for a while. She was scared to come out. She was scared of me. Can you imagine that? And if she was scared of me, I know she must of gone crazy sure enough when she found out that most of the people in this building are Jewish to boot.

My father's sister, Mable Warrick, and her husband had lived in North Philadelphia for over forty years when the following incident occurred. Maggie recalls it because it was the first time she remembered being threatened or in danger because black people could not tell she was black. Before this time Maggie would ride the bus any time she pleased. She had the habit of trying to correct black teenagers on buses when they used "foul" language. She would tell them to get up and let other people sit down. It never crossed her mind why they were always hostile and rude and told her to mind her own business.

Walking Through North Philly

Well you know, I forget I look white, I mean I don't even think about it, but I do now and I'm scared to go out in the street since Reggie had such a fit the last time I went to see your Aunt Mable when she lived in North Philly. See, I had taken the bus and I was waiting on the corner for another bus but it was too long coming. So it was only two or three blocks, so I walked. Well Reggie called me up that night and I told him that I had gone to visit Aunt Mable, and he asked me how I got there—did I go by taxi? I said, "No, I didn't go by any taxi, I took a bus, and then when the other bus didn't come I walked the other three blocks."

Well, Reggie nearly had a fit! He said, "You walked? Mama, you walked? *I never want you to walk or take the bus to North Philly again; don't you know you could have had your head knocked off?" I said, "Why? I'm not afraid of my own people." He said, "Mama, those folks don't know you are black. You don't look black to them. They don't know what you are! It doesn't matter anyhow, some of them would knock your head off if you were black as coal, much less look like you do. I don't want you to go to North Philly on the bus! I will pay for the taxi any time you want to go see Aunt Mable."*

Well, he raved and scared me to death; see, I didn't even think that my own people wouldn't know I was colored. Well, from that time on, I was very careful. I won't open my mouth on the bus or anything because I'm afraid I might say something wrong and they won't know I'm colored. I used to try to tell the black children not to use bad language, you know. But I don't do it any more.

But things are so bad now the black and white teenagers work in gangs together and wait for us to come out of the building. They don't care what color you are. They want what's in your pocketbook. It's terrible! The white ones are just as bad as the black ones. They all use the worst language, and the girls, the girls are as bad as the boys. Now we go out together early in the morning to the market, and we are home by noon. See, we have to go when we can use our passes [for those over sixty-five]. Looks like they just want to knock old people down; I think it's a shame. But I don't open my mouth. Some of them [blacks and whites] don't have any mothers to teach them, some of the mothers just don't bother to teach their children right from wrong any more. It's a sad situation when people are afraid of their own children.

When Maggie moved into the building where she now lives, one of her first friends was a white maintenance man named Clarence (a fictional name). According to Maggie, Clarence would do anything for her. He was described as full of fun and always laughing. Somehow Clarence got the nickname "Crazy

Clarence" because he was always full of fun and liked to play tricks on people. Maggie claims that Clarence was not crazy. He was simply trying to be friendly. He had a warm sense of humor and was well liked in the building. His nickname, "Crazy Clarence," was a sort of affectionate term people used to refer to him. It was a nickname that was sometimes misinterpreted by those who did not know him well.

Crazy Clarence

One day Clarence and I were riding on the same elevator. I was going downstairs to get my mail. Well, I always liked Clarence; he was always willing to do things for me, and we started talking. He told me that the reason why the elevator was so slow was because it needed to be repaired. This meant we had to get off at the fifth floor, because the elevator repairmen were waiting on the fifth floor and we had to get off and change elevators, and get on the other one.

So when we got off, the elevator men were standing there, and I never saw such tall young men in my life. So Clarence had pushed the button and the other elevator was on its way up. So I said to one of the young men, "My goodness, you are tall, it looks like you would be good basketball players." Well, he looked at me and smiled and he said, "No, Ma'am, we wouldn't have a chance, the 'niggers' got basketball all tied up." And they started joking about how the "niggers" had basketball all tied up.

I thought Clarence was going to die. He said, "Man, you should watch what you say, you shouldn't have said that, this lady is colored!" Well by that time the other elevator had come and I had gotten on and one of the men said "Go on, 'Crazy' " —they called him "Crazy Clarence," and Clarence was about crazy then; he kept yelling, "Man, you better watch what you say, you shouldn't have said that, this lady is colored, I tell you!"

Well, I said, "Come on, Clarence, you will miss the elevator." So Clarence jumped on the elevator, still fussing. He and I were on there alone, and he kept saying, "They shouldn't have said that, they shouldn't have said that." I said, "Clarence, don't worry about it!" He said, "I'm going back up there and lay them out! They shouldn't have said that!" Well, I went on and got my mail and went on up to my apartment.

Well, the next morning Clarence couldn't wait to get up to my apartment. He said, "Mrs. Lawson, wasn't that awful what those elevator men said yesterday? You know I went back down there and I told them that you were colored. They told me I was crazy, that you weren't no more colored than they were." Well, I couldn't say a word, Clarence kept repeating how awful it was that they said, "'niggers' got basketball all tied up." Then he told me they started calling him "Crazy Clarence," said "man, we heard you were crazy, now we know you are crazy."

Well, Clarence never got over that. Every time he came up here to do something, he would remind me how awful that was, he was so upset. He's not here now; I hear he's coming back though—I hope he does, because he was so nice. I hated to see him so upset like that.[17]

Maggie and her Jewish friends in the building often go to the supermarket together. It is, in a way, a meeting place for strangers who see each other enough to recognize each other, even though they do not know each other by name. Often Maggie sees the same people, and they will stop and chat about the weather and the news, and exchange pleasantries but not names. Maggie claims she had seen the women mentioned in the following story in the Penn Fruit supermarket several times. They had recognized each other, but had never talked to each other before. This day Maggie was alone. Usually she tells this story to her Jewish friends and her family.

Conversation in the Supermarket

Well, now I have become a Jew. I don't know why she mistakened me for a Jew, but she did. You know, I was standing in line at the Penn Fruit that day, and it was during the time when they caught that big Jewish politician in some trouble. It was a lot of publicity about it. It was all over the newspapers.

So we were standing there in line, and this woman was behind me. It was a long line and we started talking. So she said, "Isn't it awful?" She was talking about the Jewish politician. And I said it was awful the way politicians were so corrupt these days. So she said, "But he is a Jew. And you know we Jews have had enough trouble, haven't we? We certainly don't need this kind of trouble, do we? Aren't you ashamed to be a Jew and see another one of us do something to make us ashamed like this?"

Well, that's when I knew she thought I was Jewish too. So I said, "Yes, but we have a lot to be proud of too, don't you think?" She said yes, we did have a lot to be proud of but they would forget all about whatever we had to be proud of whenever a Jew did something wrong; it was always worse; it made it bad for the rest of us. She was sad enough so I didn't tell her I was colored. I just said, "Well, that's the truth. We certainly have had enough trouble, and it is always worse when we do something." I was thinking about Negroes, but I knew how she felt so I didn't tell her that.

Maggie often laughs at some of her memories of "color" and "race" but the following incident she took seriously. She repeats this story whenever she has the opportunity to do so.

Black Boys, White Men

A lot of people here still don't know I'm colored. Well, I'm nice to everybody, but I don't mingle downstairs much [the Game and Recreation Room].

Well, anyway, they got a new manager of maintenance; that's before they got the one they have now. And they were going to have a big meeting downstairs. It was a big affair and they had tables and seats arranged and everything. Well I wasn't going, but they convinced me to go.

Well, as things happened I was sitting right next to the new manager and he was trying to be friendly and we started talking about something. Well anyway, the subject came up about improving maintenance. He said to me, "Well, you know I think one of the problems here is we have too many black boys. You know they aren't much good when it comes to work. They don't work like the white men do. In fact, you have to keep behind them all the time. That's why they never amount to nothing."

Well, it was all I could do to sit there quiet like Kate said to do. Kate said to sit quiet and listen. So I sat still. And he said one thing that was going to change around here now that he was head of maintenance was that he was going to spend his time keeping up with those "niggers." They were really going to have to work or he was going to fire them one at a time and get some white men in here. Before the year was out there wouldn't be a "lazy nigger" left on the maintenance crew. Then he said again, "Don't you agree? They never amount to anything."

Well, he asked me a question so I had to say something. So I said, "Well, let me tell you something about 'niggers.' I haven't raised any 'niggers' myself, and I don't know anybody who has. I raised two black men and I would have raised a third one, only he died for his country in the Second World War."

Well he was sitting there not saying a word, so I said, "And another thing, I have one granddaughter who is making honors at Girls High and another one just about to finish college, and she worked three jobs and still makes the Dean's List. I know a lot of colored mothers like me who have raised black men. If I were you I would keep my mouth shut." Yes, I told him that, I certainly did. I told him, "If I were you, I would keep my mouth shut because you never know who you are talking to. Especially these days. See I'm colored and you couldn't tell that. I want you to know that I don't appreciate you calling my sons and other black men boys. It's a good thing my sons weren't here to hear you talk like that, because you would be picking yourself up in pieces looking for your teeth if you called one of my sons a black boy. My sons don't like it, and I don't either.

Now, let me ask you something else. Do you pay those black boys the same thing you pay those white men? I think that's something we ought to talk about here in this meeting tonight. You look pretty old to me to have to spend your time running around being head man, talking about 'lazy niggers.'"

I didn't give him time to answer, see, I was looking right in his face and he was speechless anyhow. So I told him that he might as well keep quiet, because he couldn't recall the spoken word, you know that's what Caddy and Kate said, you can't recall the spoken word and you can't apologize for a bad habit. So I figured he was in the habit of talking like this, and he didn't know me, so it wasn't anything he could say or do. So I shut up and just sat there, and he sat there and never looked my way. And every time they asked for new business, or suggestions or anything, I would turn my head and look at him, but he wouldn't look at me. He looked straight ahead, but I didn't open my mouth. I wasn't saying anything because I knew what I was going to do and it wasn't going to be to make a public display, because then it would be all over. See, all he would have to do was apologize and then it would have been a chance for him to tell everybody that he didn't mean it like it sounded, or something. He wouldn't have to worry about what I was going to do. So we sat there that whole meeting not saying a word. No. He didn't say a word. No. He didn't say a word, the whole meeting. Two weeks later he was gone. Fired. Yes, my friends and I took action. [18]

Maggie sees herself as being prejudiced in some respects, and she maintains that everybody else is too. I have heard time and time again, "You know if they hate Jews, they have *got* to hate blacks. You know if they hate Italians, they have *got* to hate blacks." Therefore, her strategy is usually confined to strangers or people who do not know her very well. Her strategy is to counteract prejudice against any group by immediately informing the speaker that she is a part of whatever group is under attack. If it is the Jews, she is a Jew; if it is the Italians, she is an Italian; if it is the Catholics, she is a Catholic. And there are *no exceptions*. One day I asked her about Native Americans, and she said, "Well, I just say that my grandfather was one, or my daughter is married to one, or something like that." However, when she has encountered prejudice against a group that she too is prejudiced against, she is prone to agree, sometimes aloud. When I brought this to her attention on one occasion, she excused herself on the grounds of "well, maybe not all of them are like that, *but . . .*"

One thing she did not count on: she cannot be *visibly* black when she pleases. She discovered this one day when two black women picked her pocket in the Farmers Market. Maggie was as mad as she could be. "It's terrible," she said, "when you can't even trust your *own people* to treat you right." I tried to be as gentle as possible. I said, "Maybe they thought you were white." Maggie was shocked. She was shocked in the way that she had been shocked the day one of her little black grandchildren got lost behind the candy counter in the five-and-ten-cent store. The child stayed there for two hours, sucking on a big lollipop, while Maggie had hysterics as she told the police the child had been kidnapped. Maggie told me she was about to lose her mind when she saw the child sitting behind that candy counter. She never understood why those "five-and-ten-cent dummies," as she called them, who knew they had a lost child and who knew she had a lost child, did not put two and two together. I said, "Maggie, I will make a sign to hang around your neck like the Chinese did when the government was throwing all the Japanese-Americans in jail during the War, and print in big letters, 'I AM BLACK'!" I laughed for a long time just thinking how Maggie, after all these years of using her color as she pleased, would have to hang this sign around her neck when she went to the Farmers Market.

I had forgotten about laughing at the thought of Maggie's having to wear a sign around her neck until the day I finished my graduate education. Maggie was dissatisfied with the way the ceremony had been conducted. She expected all Ph.D.'s to walk across the stage, to shake the President's hand, and to receive the degree directly from him. Instead, we had to wait about an hour, go to a tea, and get the degree from a dean.

Maggie had insisted that I keep on the gown and parade around the campus so everybody could see me and I could introduce her to everybody. I was so irritated that before we got to the tea I had snapped at Maggie about three times.

It was a hot day. Finally, we got to the tea. I got the degree, opened it. It was in Latin. I rolled it back up and was about to give it to Maggie when she said, "Let me see that thing." I gave it to her, she opened it and looked at it a long time. I said, "Well, can you read it?" I knew she could not read Latin. She looked me square in the eyes and she said, "Yes, I can. It says, "THIS IS A SMART-ASS NIGGER WHO THINKS HER NAME IS ALBERT EINSTEIN."

In an essay on Afro-American literature the black scholar and writer, Lance Jeffers, makes the following observation:

> The wholeness of all human life includes hell. . . . In Afro-American letters . . . hell is traditionally and passionately captured. Hell is racism, hell is lynching, hell is hunger, hell is poverty. . . . The black writer wrestles with this hell, chews and swallows and digests it; hellfire, devil, tail and all.[19]

Jeffers challenges the black writer not only to face hell but to look beyond it, and to have the courage to draw prophetic conclusions from its existence. Jeffers is right when he says "hell is racism." Certainly, there is nothing funny about racism. Yet in my family folklore, stories such as those presented in this part function to reduce racism to the absurd. These are what I call Maggie's stories of "color" and "race."

"Hell" is a relative concept; it is a matter of perception, a matter of degree, of moments of deep hurt before the hurt is understood. It is "God and Lice." It is Jim Crow and shoebox lunches. It is white sections and peanut galleries. It is a white-skinned black mama with a brown-skinned child who wants more than anything else a big, fat, black mammy. It is Hitler. It is Mussolini. It is the death of a son, just nineteen, fighting a war to save the world for democracy, in a segregated army. It is a white-skinned black grandmother losing a black grandchild in the five-and-ten-cent store.

It is being scared to death on a bus by a white-skinned "nigger" and jumping off the bus into a nest of "niggers." It is moving, moving, moving to get away from "niggers," to find yourself confronted with a white-skinned "nigger" whose children are all Jews. It is locking yourself in an apartment eating oranges, knowing that you are surrounded by Jews. It is wanting to be *somebody*. Working for years to be *somebody* and losing your chance to be somebody because you did not know that "urine" was the same thing as "piss" and "pee."

Maggie's stories show how Maggie tried to change the scenery in "hell"; the raw data of "hell" are covered by a cloak of the comic.

But the images of hell persist; we see that all the personal "hells" in Maggie's stories are created by the same invisible monster. It is a monster of negative thoughts about people we have yet to know, a monster made up of negative stereotypes, race, skin color. It shoves millions of human beings into inferior and superior categories, and the invisible monster is lurking, stalking, waiting to warp the minds of our children, all of our children, be they "white," "red," "black," "yellow," or "brown."[20] This is the prophetic message of Maggie's stories.

Afterword

by Otey M. Scruggs

Kathryn L. Morgan's *Children of Strangers* is personal experience raised to the level of a group experience that speaks to the human condition. The central concern of these stories is the quality of that experience: how people have coped with life in the process of shaping relations with other people. If the Dardens, in the entertaining and useful book *Spoonbread and Strawberry Wine*, which invites comparison in black family history with *Children of Strangers*, offer us recipes for cooking, Professor Morgan offers us a recipe for coping. Black people, she pointedly contends, have had to construct "buffers," internal coping mechanisms, in order to deal effectively with the "hell of racism," with life in all its tragicomic absurdity, in all its complexity. Professor Morgan offers ample support to Albert Murray's assertion in his provocative *The Omni-Americans* that "slavery and oppression may well have made black people more human and more American while it has made white people less human and less American."[1]

The "hell of racism" hovers over all the stories, even those comprising Part II, which focuses less on slavery and oppression and more on manners and morals. For tales inculcating such values as discipline, punctuality, common sense, and Christian faith were designed to reinforce those larger goals of respect-

I am indebted to my brother-in-law, Professor Lawrence C. Howard, Graduate School of Public and International Affairs, University of Pittsburgh, for his love of conversation from which I have benefitted more times than I can remember.

ability and responsibility that a people intent upon countering negative images of themselves have assiduously cultivated. The Stepin Fetchit image was as much detested in our home as in Morgan's. The "hunched over" walk was my father's pet passion. An ex-soldier, veteran of 24th Infantry Regiment duty in the Philippines before World War I and a labor battalion in France during the war, Father had a walk that was distinctly military: body erect, chin up, eyes straight ahead, knees pumping slightly and arms swinging easily at his sides. One day during my boyhood, we were walking along, I slightly hunched, with hands in pocket, when suddenly he whirled and yelled, "Take your hands out of your pockets, boy, and stand up straight!" Today, nearly thirty years after his death, his walk remains one of my most vivid memories of him. And I suspect he would be hard-pressed to conceal his irritation with me, for I have remained a hands-in-pocket "stroller," not a straight-up "marcher." Unquestionably, several generations of black families have been weaned on such martial training. In her excellent family biography, *Proud Shoes*, Pauli Murray tells of her Grandfather Fitzgerald, Union Army veteran, teaching his daughters to walk "like soldiers." "'Wait a minute, children,'" he would say to them as they moved along, "'We're out of step. Now, *left*, right, *left*, right,' and from two to five daughters would swing forward with him in military stride, flanking him on each side and stepping high, long voluminous skirts swirling about their ankles, shoulders back and heads up in the air."[2] The special "hell" Professor Morgan refers to is the intrusion of stereotypes of race and color into so many aspects of black people's daily lives.

As pointed up in *Children of Strangers*, the "hell of racism" has larger significance: the inter-connection of black and white. The historical experience of the Gordon-Carson household affords us ample evidence of the ubiquity of blackness in America. Albert Murray was not engaging in empty rhetoric when he wrote that "U.S. Negroes represent a composite of all images.

No other segment of the population of the United States encompasses more of the nation's limitless variety, whether in physical appearance or in behavior. Indeed, perhaps the most significant and scientifically supportable observation to be made about native-born U.S. Negroes as a *race* is that they may be by way of becoming a new racial (i.e., physical) type, perhaps the only one that is truly indigenous, so to speak to contemporary North America."[3]

It is clear that the origins of millions of American black people are racially mixed. It should be equally clear, were it not for the silence that has enveloped the issue, that the same is true of whites. The pilgrimage of the Gordons' white-skinned Carson cousins who "crossed over" has been standard. Pauli Murray's Uncle Billy, for example, as well as the history of this writer's family, abundantly attest to the large volume of movement across the color line. However, most whites have sought to deny the blackness that is such an integral part of their American lineage. In so doing they have cut themselves off from a potentially rich racial and cultural identity, in effect committing racial suicide. Maggie was surely aware of the connection between recognition of one's identity and life itself. Comfortable with her own identity, a racial blend, Maggie's custom was to invite friends of all races and backgrounds to her Philadelphia home, prompting some of her black neighbors to refer to it as Lepersville. (The idea leprosy evokes is nothing if not death.) And when whites clung to their hatred of blackness and to their attachment to whiteness after World War II, Morgan tells us that her mother became less accepting and more openly critical of their racial provincialism. But, then, the Gordons had always "kept the color."

Maggie's black identity was also reinforced when in the process of "passing" she was relating to whites. This, of course, is not primarily a book about passing. Much of the time Maggie makes no conscious effort to be white; she is simply taken for white. Mistaken identity, however, enables her to hear what white people hear when they are thinking about blacks (in addition to getting her into occasional difficulties with blacks). At the same time, white readers especially are being made privy to how a black person reacts to what whites are thinking. Maggie can fiercely defend her race or lay back, depending on her assessment of the situation. Such sophisticated behavior is as true a test of positive feelings about one's identity as can be devised. Here is no "tragic mulatto," a "marginal" character out of a second-rate novel whose total lack of identity can only perpetuate racism. To the black reader, Maggie symbolizes racial solidarity. Whatever the opportunities, light-skinned blacks will not abandon those whose lot is cast with the Negro group. My Aunt Dora, my mother's sister, did pass (what chance did she have of obtaining a clerical job with the City of Los Angeles in the 1920's if she had declared herself Negro?). With Mother, however, discussion of passing was quite simply taboo.

Albert Murray once made the astute comment that identity is better defined in cultural than in racial terms. And he went on to observe that "American culture, even in its most rigidly segregated precincts, is patently and irrevocably composite. It is, regardless of all the hysterical protestations of those who would have it otherwise, *incontestably mulatto.*"[4] Rooted in Southern soil, the black component has followed the movement of Negroes, whether to Philadelphia or to California, where I was born and raised. The truth is that the cultural experience of the Gordons has had much in common with that of hundreds of thousands of black families. Caddie and Kate and Albert and Maggie and Kathryn and the others are to me familiar people. No doubt, this identification has been facilitated by my family's Virginia origins. My father came from a large, close-knit family of small-farm owners near Roanoke, not far from the Gordon's native Lynchburg. He, like them, was part of the large migration of black people from the state between 1900 and the Great Depression. Born a slave in Virginia of black, red, and white ancestry, my maternal grandmother at age twelve, in 1862, took her African-Cherokee mother and escaped to the North. By all accounts, she, like Caddie, was a shrewd, down-to-earth, strong-willed woman who valued industry, education, and property-ownership. I doubt not that like Caddie she had little regard for "white trash." But there was no talk of white "aristocratic blood." Indeed, according to my Cousin Anita, when greeted with the question of ancestry grandmother was fond of the saying: "In the hangman's house one does not speak of rope!" The slavery experience was no more a topic of conversation in my family than in others like it. One of my paternal cousins, who still lives in Roanoke, probably put it as well as anyone when she said to me that "back in those days our parents would not tell us much about themselves. I guess they thought it was not our business to know or either they did not care to discuss it to us fearing that we would feel sorry for ourselves growing up in the public eye." Unless a "good" face could be put on such a demeaning experience, silence, too, could be a powerful "buffer."

And so these folk held strongly to the belief in self-improvement: "God helps those who help themselves" was my father's favorite maxim. Exercising considerable ingenuity, they worked at a lot of jobs to make ends meet. They inculcated in their children a strict moral code: Morgan compares Maggie's "don'ts" with the *Egyptian Negative Confessions*. They maintained a deep commitment to God: "The Lord moves in mysterious ways, his wonders to perform," my Aunt Mamie was fond of saying. Yet in spite of all this, these people have harbored a somewhat irreverent attitude toward life in response to its daily ironies and absurdities. In essence, however, this reflects a profound respect *for* life. Sharp-tongued Caddie could tell her former mistress to "Kiss my ass"; years later she pungently related to her progeny her stories of slavery, which in turned were cleaned up by her more puritanical descendants. Pauli Murray's grandmother could "bless out" her "trashy" neighbors to their great amusement and her own satisfaction.[5] Interestingly, there seems to have been an unusual number of flat-iron hurlers, actual and potential, among these families. Mama Darden, provoked by one of her daughters, once threw an iron at the wall, accidentally hitting the girl and knocking her unconscious.[6] My mother, who took in ironing, occasionally threatened to pitch a flat-iron at my sister or me if we continued to "torment" her. For her brief torment, Kate once let fly an iron at Maggie, who had returned from school a few minutes late. Here are down-to-earth people, often pressured but gifted with a large fund of common sense, people not easily taken in by the pretensions, arrogance, and hypocrisy of blacks or whites. Like Caddie, my father, who in his younger days had been a pillar in the church, came to have little regard for "preachers and church-going hypocrites." Nor was Maggie about to endure silently some snippy remark from her irritated daughter challenging her to read the Latin on Kathryn's newly received Ph.D. degree. "It says," retorted Maggie, "'THIS IS A SMART ASS NIGGER WHO THINKS HER NAME IS ALBERT EINSTEIN.'" This is biting humor, the kind that would have brought forth from such as my father gales of laughter (as it does from me). It is the kind of put-down which had it been administered to me by my practical, no-nonsense father would have quickly punctured my sometimes inflated ego. As Professor Morgan makes abundantly clear, these stories were designed to appeal to the common sense of their listeners, as they were sometimes designed to appeal to their sense of guilt. In their intent to instruct as well as to entertain, they provided guides to conduct and spurs to ambition. There were lessons to be learned here, morals to be drawn, as my father used to say, by anyone who had not "lost the sense he was born with." And as Pauli Murray has said about her family's lore: "It was through these homespun stories, each with its own moral, that my elders sought to build their family traditions."[7]

The most significant aspect of black culture for present purposes is the art of storytelling. Of the blues, Albert Murray has written: "As an art form, the blues idiom by its very nature goes beyond the objective of making human existence bearable physically and psychologically. The most elementary and hence the least dispensable objective of all serious artistic expression, whether aboriginal or sophisticated, is to make human existence *meaningful*. Man's primary concern with life is to make it as significant as possible, and the blues are part of this effort."[8] It seems to me that what Murray is saying about the blues can be applied with equal force to the art of storytelling. Both are concerned with extending human possibilities. Both are part of the African-American oral tradition. People like Caddie and Maggie and Grandfather Fitzgerald and my father and Cousin Anita are artists with the spoken word. Though many are far removed from slavery and Southern rural and small-town life, and some never experienced them, and though many are highly literate, these people have retained a native skill with the spoken word. The rhythms and idioms and tones, which is to say the style of the language, sometimes evoke pathos but more often laughter.

It scarcely need be said that what W. E. B. Du Bois referred to as the Negro's gift of laughter has contributed importantly to his ability to cope. Interestingly, Langston Hughes' only novel (Hughes told very amusing stories and was a literary master of black folk idiom) bore the title, *Not Without Laughter*. Self-humor, as Professor Morgan terms it (for black people can easily turn it on themselves), is beautifully captured in Maggie's splendidly ironic statement: "If some white woman had done to 'Miss Mary' what 'Miss Mary' did to Marie, 'Miss Mary' would be hustling down to the NAACP with her coattails flapping in the wind, yelling prejudice to the top of her lungs!" Here is enough wisdom put metaphorically for a month of days. Dependent upon the inflection in the sound, the meaning of the language—the humor and irony—can not be fully appreciated without hearing its expression. Perhaps because my father came from the same locale in Virginia as the Gordons, Maggie's language has to me the ring of familiarity.

My father was an accomplished storyteller. I would gladly settle for half his gift. Like Grandfather Fitzgerald, many of his tales were about his military experience, emphasizing the warrior values of heroism and courage. Like many a raconteur, for such he was, he was not averse to stretching the truth, occasionally even running roughshod over it. Though not in accord with the records, which I discovered many years later, Father often claimed to have served on the southwestern border playing hide-and-seek with Pancho Villa. But he knew more than enough history to make such an assertion seem plausible. And like many a fine storyteller, too, he appreciated a good tale well told. Often his reaction to such stories was, "Your people! Your people!" Sometimes the declaration was accompanied by a look of utter disgust. More often, however, his reaction was one of wonderment. Shaking his head, Father would rock with laughter. What foolish things Negroes sometimes do, he seemed to be saying. But how inventive they are in coping with the absurdities of race. He would certainly have found Professor Morgan's story of Philadelphia, the "Titty" of Brotherly Love, where a woman's "titty hung down to her knees," a real rib-tickler as well as a tale pointing up the pervasiveness of racism of the kind he encountered all his life. Their circumstances, as Professor Morgan implies throughout the book, required all the capacity for humor and laughter these migrants from the Southern countryside could muster. Humor has served an important function: it has cushioned the transition to urban living.

Children of Strangers is an historical document. A unique resource, it contains raw materials for social and cultural history. And it comes at a time when the study of family history is growing in importance. It informs us of some very significant happenings in a black family from the Civil War to the present. And as such, it should help explode the myth of the monolithic black family or the myth that social class overshadows whatever similarities families may have. The book thus points up the confusion surrounding the use by "social science technicians" of a concept like social class. Despite the stress placed by such families as the Gordons on values generally considered "middle-class," *Children of Strangers* portrays a large, cohesive family rising above class and color. The important thing is that such families share with the majority of blacks an attitude, a way of viewing life, that is irreverent, almost defiant, that is sharply punctuated by a sense of laughter and the need "to make human existence meaningful." As badly off as black people have been in this country, whatever their background they have been able to transcend their predicament and laugh at themselves and the inane in human affairs. That is no small accomplishment. No people with such a sense of the absurd, regardless of their "middle-class" values and aspirations, could be as out of touch with each other as some "social science technicians," preoccupied with class distinctions, would have us believe. At the heart of *Children of Strangers*, it seems to me, is this message: the black experience in America speaks directly to the "limitless variety" of American experience. Could it be that the Gordons of this country are leading the way in rich-textured, complex living which in the final analysis is the essence of the good life?

Writers, social scientists, folklorists, historians, biographers and other scholars—all have dealt with such subjects as slavery, racism, color, migration, passing, and urbanization. Pauli Murray, for example, employs family stories and anecdotes as historical tools in her splendid family biography, *Proud Shoes*, a piece of work beautifully and sensitively fashioned. The uniqueness of *Children of Strangers* is that it directs our attention to all of these issues while it permits us to glimpse how members of one family see themselves and their ancestors, not through the intermediation of the historian, but through their own eyes. As more oral histories and accounts like *Children of Strangers* accumulate, larger strides will be taken toward the construction of historical generalizations about black families that will go far to undermine the myths.

General readers as well as scholars should benefit from reading this book. Instructive and entertaining, the stories have been written with more than a passing eye at the general reader. Hopefully, many who read them will be moved to collect their own family lore, for their own satisfaction and the edification of others. *Children of Strangers* should provide badly needed encouragement and inspiration to blacks and whites in the age-old struggle for a more humane existence.

Otey M. Scruggs
Syracuse, New York
July 26, 1980

Notes

Preface

1. James M. Lacy, "Folklore of the South and Racial Discrimination," *Publications of the Texas Folklore Society* 32 (1958): 101–102.
2. Martin Luther King, Jr., "Letter from Birmingham Jail," in Leslie H. Fishel and Benjamin Quarles, eds., *The Black American: A Documentary History* (Glenview, Ill., 1976; orig. pub. 1967), p. 522.
3. Saunders Redding, *On Being Negro in America* (New York, 1962), p. 81.
4. Ernest J. Gaines, "The Sky Is Grey," *Negro Digest* 12 (1963): 86.
5. B. A. Botkin, ed., *Lay My Burden Down: A Folk History of Slavery* (Chicago, 1965); Richard M. Dorson, *Negro Tales from Pine Bluff, Arkansas, and Calvin, Michigan* (Bloomington, Ind., 1958), pp. 110–127.
6. James Baldwin, *Nobody Knows My Name* (New York, 1961), p. 73.
7. John O. Killens, *Black Man's Burden* (Pocket Book ed., New York, 1969; orig. pub. 1965), p. 76.
8. W. E. B. Du Bois, *The World and Africa: An Inquiry into the Part Which Africa Has Played in World History* (enlarged ed., New York, 1965; orig. pub. 1947), p. 149.
9. Lawrence W. Levine, *Black Culture and Black Consciousness* (New York, 1977), p. ix.; Alan Dundes, ed., *Mother Wit from the Laughing Barrel* (Englewood Cliffs, 1973), p. 595; Alex Haley, "Black History, Oral History, and Genealogy," *Oral History Review* 7 (1973): 1; Gladys Marie Frye, *Night Riders in Black Folk History* (Nashville, 1975), pp. 212–215.
10. Interview with researchers from Educational Film Center of North Springfield, Virginia, summer 1979.

Caddy and Family History

1. On the subject of "passing," see C. Eric Lincoln, "Color, Race and Group Identity in the United States," *Daedalus* 96 (1967): 527–541.
2. Similar slave narratives can be found in B. A. Botkin, ed., *Lay My Burden Down* (Chicago, 1961). For references to children being sold on the block, see "Cato—Alabama," p. 86, "Joanna Draper—Mississippi," p.

98, "Katie Rowe—Arkansas," p. 105. For an account of the extreme cruelty of whippings, see "Story of Ben Simpson," p. 75.

3. See Botkin, ed., pp. 223–253, for many accounts of the reactions of slaves and their owners when they heard of the Emancipation Proclamation. See "They Danced All Night," p. 226, "He Cussed Till He Died," p. 233, and "Death of a Plantation," pp. 235–236.

4. "Cato—Alabama" recalls that "They was the best quality white folks and they was always good to me, 'cause I's one of their blood. . . . That's what makes me so mixed up with Indians, African and white blood. Sometimes it mattered to me, sometimes it didn't. It don't no more 'cause I'm not too far from the end of my days" (Botkin, ed., pp. 84–85).

5. For references to the various standards used for Negro class structure, see E. Franklin Frazier, *Black Bourgeoisie* (Glencoe, Ill., 1949); Richard Bardolph, *The Negro Vanguard* (New York, 1961). For a description of marriage customs among slaves, see Botkin, ed., "Tines Kendricks—Georgia," p. 70.

6. For another account of self-defense, see Richard M. Dorson, *Negro Tales from Pine Bluff, Arkansas, and Calvin, Michigan* (Bloomington, Ind., 1958), "Will Kimbro Defends Himself," pp. 230–232. For traditional themes concerning the Negro's fight for his rights, see Botkin, ed., "The Slave's Chance," pp. 174–178.

Our Childhood

1. For the viewpoints of ex-slaves who described the naming practices after "freedom" often objected to them, see Fisk University, *Unwritten History of Slavery* (Microcard ed., Washington, D.C., 1968; orig. pub. 1945), p. 20; Norman R. Yetman, ed., *Life Under the Peculiar Institution*, "Lorenzo Ezell—Texas," p. 112, "Lizzie Williams—North Carolina," p. 319. For academic interpretations of black naming practices during and after enslavement, see Alan Dundes, ed., *Mother Wit from the Laughing Barrel* (Englewood Cliffs, 1973), pp. 142–174. For a graphic description of a romance between two ex-slaves, see Yetman, ed., "Lucy Ann Dunn—North Carolina," p. 102, and "Peter Clifton—South Carolina," p. 59. A reference to naming practices in Lynchburg in the 1930s is in Works Progress Administration (WPA), *The Negro in Virginia*, p. 346.

2. For whippings and other child-rearing practices among black families during and after enslavement, see Fisk University, pp. 68–69, and Gladys Marie Frye, *Night Riders in Black Folk History* (Nashville, 1975), p. 58.

3. For a historical treatment of the role of churches in Virginia at the turn of the century, see WPA, pp. 247–262.

4. For values and the "gift of ownership," see WPA, pp. 215–225.
5. An interesting account of how he tried to learn to read by using the blue-back spelling book is given by Henry Johnson of Missouri in Yetman, p. 184. My mother still has the copy used by Albert, called the New York Spelling Book; pages 1–13 are missing. The book has been sewn together and it still has some of Albert's scribbling in it. For an insightful analysis of the value of education, land, family unity, and home ownership in Virginia, see WPA, pp. 215–225.
6. One reference to "educated fools" may be found in Fisk University, p. 73.
7. For an insightful discussion of tensions between Southern blacks and those blacks who move north and return south to visit, see John O. Killens, *Black Man's Burden* (Pocket Book ed., New York, 1969; orig. pub. 1965), pp. 61–96. For comments on black humor, see Langston Hughes, "Jokes Negroes Tell on Themselves," *Negro Digest* 9 (1965): 21–25; Alan Dundes, ed., pp. 649–669; Lawrence W. Levine, *Black Culture and Black Consciousness* (New York, 1977), pp. 307–344.
8. For a similar story, see Frye, pp. 80–81.
9. See Carroll Y. Rich, "Born with the Veil: Black Folklore in Louisiana," *Journal of American Folklore* 89 (1976): 328–331, and Loudell F. Snow, "I Was Born Exactly with the Gift," *Journal of American Folklore* 86 (1973): 272–281.
10. For a similar story, see Fisk University, p. 30.

Maggie's Stories of "Color" and "Race"

1. For the "poor mulatto" theme in novels, see Geoffrey Barnes, *Dark Lustre* (New York, 1932); Fannie Hurst, *Imitation of Life* (New York, 1933); Julia Peterkin, *Bright Skin* (Dunwoody, Ga., 1932); James Weldon Johnson, *The Autobiography of an Ex-Colored Man* (New York, 1912); William Wells Brown, *Clotelle, or The President's Daughter* (1867). For additional references see Sterling A. Brown, *Negro Poetry and Drama* (New York, 1969; orig. pub. 1937). For a discussion of films dealing with family conflicts caused by the ambivalence of white-skinned black family members, see Donald Woods, *Toms, Coons, Mulattoes, Mammies, and Blacks* (New York, 1973), pp. 339–340. Woods gives a brief description of *Imitation of Life* and *Pinky*. For a critical review of Hurst's *Imitation of Life,* see Sterling A. Brown, "Imitation of Life: Once a Pancake," *Opportunity* 13 (1935): 87.
2. For additional information on color differences within black families in Virginia, see Works Progress Administration. (WPA), *The Negro in Virginia,* pp. 84–85. Especially significant is the reference on page 223 to

Skeeter-Town, established in the colonial period by free white-skinned blacks. After the Civil War the residents of Skeeter-Town welcomed ex-slaves of all complexions and sold them land.

3. Quoted in Joel A. Rogers, *Sex and Race,* vol. 1 (New York, 1967; orig. pub. 1941), p. 1.

4. For similar incidents on Jim Crow coaches see WPA, pp. 241–242. For additional accounts of blacks who pass for white or who have been mistaken for white in the 1940s, see Joel A. Rogers, *Nature Knows No Color Line* (New York, 1952), pp. 200–203, 215; Rayford W. Logan, "Confessions of an Unwilling Nordic," in Sterling Brown, Arthur P. Davis, and Ulysses Lee, eds., *The Negro Caravan* (New York, 1970; orig. pub. 1941), pp. 1043–1050. Logan states that even though he did not look white, because of his credentials he was presumed to be white by the U. S. Army and was assigned as an officer in a white unit overseas during the Second World War. He makes reference to his brother, who could "pass" and who refused to be seen with him on one occasion. Logan concludes that he is opposed to segregation in any form but if a law were passed requiring "all anomalous Negroes to wear on their exterior garments and on the windshield of their automobiles a sign "colored" I should comply most willingly."

5. Walter White, "I Investigate Lynching," in Brown, Davis, and Lee, eds., pp. 1005–1017. Walter White is described by the editors as a "voluntary" black.

6. C. Eric Lincoln, "Color, Race and Group Identity in the United States," *Daedalus* 96 (1967): 527–541.

7. For reactions in Harlem, see John O. Killens, *Black Man's Burden* (Pocket Book ed., New York, 1969; orig. pub. 1965), p. 113; Lawrence W. Levine, *Black Culture and Black Consciousness* (New York, 1977), pp. 420–440.

8. John Hope Franklin, *From Slavery to Freedom* (New York, 1974; orig. pub. 1947), p. 436. From the black perspective, Joe Louis's fights and the invasion of Ethiopia were examples of blacks versus whites. In fact, the United States, Nazi Germany, and Italy were allies in the perpetuation of the white supremacy doctrines. It was not until Hitler proclaimed the Germans to be the "master race" and reduced all other white races to inferior status that the American writings supporting white supremacy declined.

9. Rogers, vol. 1, p. 20.

10. Franklin, p. 435.

11. For additional testimony from whites who passed for black, see Joel A. Rogers, *Sex and Race,* vol. 2 (New York, 1972; orig. pub. 1942), pp.

372–373, 378–379. For references to "a white lady" who was passing for black, see Joel A. Rogers, *Sex and Race*, vol. 3 (New York, 1972; orig. pub. 1944), p. 301. For an entire community that passed for black to escape the penalties for intermarriage in Lee County, Louisiana, in 1908, see Rogers, vol. 3, p. 22.

12. In the North my mother is called "Marge" by her friends. She is called "Marjorie" in the North and "Maggie" in the South.

13. Quoted in Gordon W. Allport, *The Nature of Prejudice* (Reading, Mass., 1954), p. 148.

14. Jean Toomer, *Cane* (First Perennial Classic ed., New York, 1969; orig. pub. 1923), p. 112.

15. For an insightful article on the effects of "color" and "race" on white behavior, see Chester Peirce, "Offensive Mechanisms," in Floyd B. Barbour, ed., *The Black Seventies* (Boston, 1970), pp. 265–282. Peirce is a black psychiatrist on the Faculty of Medicine at Harvard University. His article is particularly significant in that he offers a *solution* to the problem. For other views of the effects of "color" and "race" on behavior, see also Alan Dundes, ed., *Mother Wit from the Laughing Barrel* (Englewood Cliffs, 1973), pp. 9–21; Eric Berne, "The Mythology of Dark and Fair: Psychiatric Use of Folklore," *Journal of American Folklore* (1959): 1–13.

16. According to my mother, her reference to "Stella Dallas" was to an old motion picture about a "cheap-looking" white woman. She uses the term "Stella Dallas" to denote a white woman who in her opinion wears too much makeup, cheap jewelry, or flashy clothes. On the validity of considering recent narratives transmitted orally in traditional form as materials of folklore and history, see Stephen Zeitlin, ed., "I'd Like To Think They Were Pirates . . ." (Washington, D.C., 1975), pp. 1–33.

17. Another taped version is in "The Storytellers" in the archives of the Educational Film Center, North Springfield, Virginia.

18. Another taped version is in "The Storytellers" in the archives of the Educational Film Center, North Springfield, Virginia.

19. Lance Jeffers, "The Death of the Defensive Posture: Toward Grandeur in Afro-American Letters," in Barbour, ed., p. 258. Jeffers calls attention to the significance of folklore and folk traditions as sources for insights into black perceptions and world-views. For a discussion of the value of oral traditions for insights into black family life, see Courtney Brown, "Oral History and the Oral Tradition of Black America: The Kinte Foundation," *Oral History Review* 7 (1973): 26–28.

20. Margaret Walker in "Religion, Poetry and History, Foundations for a New Educational System," in Barbour, ed., p. 291, argues that it is equally

important to educate white children to value black folkways as it is to educate black children. The idea that black culture and history should be taught only to blacks would deprive white children of the possibility of escaping provincialism and distorted history.

Afterword
by Otey M. Scruggs

1. Albert M. Murray, *The Omni-Americans: New Perspectives on Black Experience and American Culture* (New York, 1970), p. 36.
2. Pauli Murray, *Proud Shoes: The Story of an American Family* (Spartansburg, S.C., 1973; orig. pub. 1956), pp. 17–18.
3. Murray, *Omni-Americans*, p. 53. Italics in original.
4. Ibid., p. 22. Italics mine.
5. Murray, *Proud Shoes*, p. 13–23.
6. Norma Jean Darden, *Spoonbread and Strawberry Wine* (New York, 1980; orig. pub. 1978), p. 29.
7. Murray, *Proud Shoes*, p. 246.
8. Murray, *Omni-Americans*, p. 58. Italics in original.